STRANGE BUT TRUE

Spontaneous Combustion

STRANGE BUT TRUE

Spontaneous Combustion

DAMON WILSON

· PARRAGON ·

This edition published and distributed by
Parragon
Unit 13–17, Avonbridge Trading Estate
Atlantic Road
Avonmouth
Bristol, BS11 9QD

This edition produced by Magpie Books, an imprint
of Robinson Publishing Ltd. in 1997

Illustrations courtesy of Popperfoto, Fortean Picture Library,
Mary Evans Picture Library

British Library Cataloguing-in-Publication Data
A catalogue record for this book is available
from the British Library

ISBN 0–75252–133–0

Printed and bound in the E.C.

Contents

1

Mrs Reeser Turns to Ash

At 9.00 p.m. on the evening of July 1, 1951, Mrs Pansy Carpenter – owner of the Allamanda Apartments in St Petersburg, Florida – paid a call on one of her residents, Mrs Mary Reeser. This 67-year-old widow had only recently moved from Pennsylvania and found the Florida heat oppressive. When Mrs Carpenter wished her goodnight she was sitting near the open window with two electric fans augmenting the gentle night breeze. Asked how she felt, Mrs Reeser assured her landlady that, apart from feeling too hot to sleep, she was perfectly well.

At 5.00 a.m. the next morning, Mrs Carpenter awoke to a loud thump, rather like a door slamming. She went to investigate but could not find the source. However, as she moved through the apartment block, she did notice a strange smell in the air which reminded her of an "over-heating electric motor." Thinking her electric water heater might be playing up again, Mrs Carpenter went to the garage, switched the unit's power off and returned to bed.

The odd smell had gone when she answered the door to a Western Union telegram messenger at 8.00 a.m. The boy had tried to deliver a message to Mrs Reeser's apartment, but had received no reply. Mrs Carpenter signed for the message and, feeling anxious, took it down the hall herself. When her knocking brought no result, Mrs Carpenter grasped the door handle to let herself in but before she could turn it she gave a shriek and staggered back flapping her hand – the metal of the knob was too hot to hold.

A few moments later, two house painters from across the street responded to Mrs Carpenter's calls for help and shouldered the door open. A blast of heat held the men back for a moment, but through a haze of super-heated air they made out what was left of Mary Reeser.

The "robust" woman, the well-stuffed armchair she had been sitting in and the side table beside it had been reduced to a pile of fine ash, interspersed with black-ened, heat-eroded chair springs. The carpet was burned away in a six-foot wide circle around the woman's remains. The ashes were still glowing red but nothing else had been burned. Stranger yet, although the apartment contained a large amount of smoke, it carried no stench of burnt flesh – just the odd, almost sweet odor Mrs Carpenter had noted earlier.

Firemen arrived within minutes and as soon as they were certain there was no further risk of fire, they examined the scene. The state of the apartment only baffled them further. Throughout the room, a moist, slightly sticky black soot coated everything above a line four feet from the floor. Below that demarcation, the room was virtually undamaged – only the wall paint immediately behind the chair in which Mrs Reeser had "gone up in smoke" was slightly browned by heat. Plastic fittings above the smoke-line were melted like candle wax, but a pile of newspapers just outside the

Mary Hardy Reeser

scorched "circle of death" were not even browned. A mirror had cracked, apparently from the heat, but Mrs Reeser's bed linen was as spotless as if it had just been made.

In the circular blaze area itself (firemen told reporters), they found a few pounds of a powdery "crisp ash," a few pieces of calcined vertebrae, a skull "shrunk uniformly to the size of an orange," and an object that resembled a dehydrated liver. Just outside the area of burned carpet was a severed, but "wholly untouched left foot still wearing its slipper." When weighed, the whole lot – including the remains of the chair and side table – came to less than ten pounds. Mrs Reeser had weighed 170 to 175 pounds. The missing 165 pounds was spread through the apartment in the form of water vapor and the greasy black soot that coated everything above four feet from the ground.

The police naturally suspected suicide or foul play. It seemed highly unlikely that a human body could burn so thoroughly with only nightclothes, a chair, a table and a bit of carpet to fuel the blaze. It seemed probable that Mrs Reeser, or somebody else, had poured fuel on the fire – therefore the remains were sent to the FBI Forensics Laboratory in Virginia and detectives looked into Mrs Reeser's circumstances.

Mary Hardy Purdy was born in 1884 in Pennsylvania, and had married a local doctor called Richard Reeser. Dr Reeser had maintained a thriving practice up to his death in 1947 and had left Mary plenty of money. Four years into her widowhood, Mary moved to St Petersburg to be near to her son Richard Jr, who was also a physician. She had been living there only five weeks when she died.

Clearing up after Mrs Reeser's Spontaneous Combustion in Florida

Friends described Mary Reeser as a kindly, gregarious person whose only faults were a streak of vanity and a rebellious stubbornness when crossed. At the time of her death, she was trying to arrange a temporary move back to Pennsylvania to escape the Florida summer heat. Unfortunately, her attempts to rent a second flat had been obstructed by several unexpected difficulties and delays. Mary had complained that these problems had depressed her, but she certainly didn't seem unhappy enough to burn herself to death. Besides, if this was a case of suicide, what had happened to the fuel container? Either it had itself been thoroughly burned-up or a second party had removed it.

As to homicide, the apartment had not been robbed and showed no sign of forced entry or a struggle. The old lady had no enemies who might want to kill her and Mrs Carpenter and the other residents had heard nothing unusual during the night other than a single thump at 5.00 a.m. Mary Reeser's son Richard had stood to gain financially by her death, and had been with her on the evening before she died, but he seemed an unlikely suspect. He was comfortably off himself and did not need his mother's money. Furthermore, he and his mother had a happy and loving relationship and there had been no quarrels.

Finally, considering the extreme localization of the blaze, it was estimated that whatever had fuelled the fire had not been poured on all at once as it would have splashed and spread. Besides, a single coating of petrol or even napalm would have done little more than blacken Mrs Reeser's skin and destroy her extremities. Therefore, investigators reasoned, a large amount of fuel must have been added gradually over a period. Nobody wanted to believe that the young Dr Reeser had stood sprinkling fuel over his burning mother for several hours.

Another homicide scenario considered by the investigators was that Mrs Reeser could have been taken to a crematorium and brought back later in the form of ashes. But the time factor ruled it out. Transporting her to the crematorium (many miles away), cremating her, returning the ashes and covering the walls with soot would certainly have taken more than ten or 11 hours.

The FBI lab's report increased the confusion. There were no traces of anything like petrol or paraffin in Mrs Reeser's ashes. In the lab's opinion, the blaze that incinerated the widow had burned unassisted. This also precluded crematorium gas jets and chemical fuels such as those found in incendiary bombs.

Investigators turned their attention to the well-stuffed armchair that had burned with Mrs Reeser. Perhaps the makers had used some highly inflammable material. The Jacksonville firm that was responsible replied indignantly that the only materials used were wood, metal springs and cotton padding. They insisted that none of the components had been treated with flammable chemicals and the chair conformed to all State safety standards. Fire experts confirmed that the chair was no more flammable than others of the same type, and that under no circumstances could it have produced the long-lasting, intense blaze necessary to cremate Mrs Reeser.

Detectives even considered the possibility of a freak lightning bolt – but even lightning would not have produced the observed effects. Death by lightning stops the heart but it does not reduce the victim to ashes. Besides, no sign of a lightning strike could be found around the apartment – the windowsills were unscorched and the electric fuses had not blown (as they almost certainly would have if a large electrical discharge had struck the building.)

The public was naturally fascinated by the mystery and bombarded the police with bizarre suggestions, such as divine vengeance or demonic attack. There was also an anonymous postcard from a man who claimed to be an eyewitness. It declared, "a ball of fire came through the open window and hit her. I seen it happen."

It was Dr Lemoyne Snyder, medico-legal director for the Michigan State Police, who offered the most plausible suggestion so far – that Mrs Reeser had fuelled the blaze with her own body fat. In his book *Homicide Investigations*, he had stated, "underneath the skin is a layer of fat which may be quite thick in heavy individuals. This burns readily, and the destruction of the tissue after a comparatively small fire may be great."

On August 8, 1951, the St Petersburg police issued a statement: "There is conclusive evidence that the deceased body could be consumed by fire, as in this case, if the body had become ignited. . . . Due to the fact that Mrs Reeser had taken a considerable amount of sedatives that night . . . . there is every possibility that Mrs Reeser, while sitting in an overstuffed chair in her apartment, could have become drowsy or fallen asleep while smoking a cigarette, thus igniting her clothes. At that time she was clad in a rayon acetate nightgown and a housecoat. The nightgown, being highly inflammable, could have been ignited by a burning cigarette, causing immediate death, if the deceased was in a semi-conscious condition.

"Naturally, when her clothes became afire they would also set the chair afire creating intense heat which completely destroyed the chair and nearby end table. Once the body became ignited, almost complete destruction occurred from the burning of its own fatty tissues. For once the body starts to burn, there is enough fat and inflammable substances to permit varying amounts of destruction to take place. Sometimes this destruction by burning will proceed to a degree which results in almost complete combustion of the body, as in this case."

The Roman philosopher, Pliny the Elder (23–79 AD), noted two cases of "sudden fire" in humans in his 37 volume book, *Natural History*. He wrote that "a light fire shone out of [the] head" of a boy called Servius Tullius, who nevertheless survived and later became the sixth king of Rome. Less fortunate was General Lucius Marcius in 212 BC, when "a flaming fire of the same sort" engulfed his head and killed him while he was exhorting his troops.

Pliny's contemporaries doubtless thought these fires were acts of the gods, as they did the philosopher's own death when he was suffocated when sailing too close to the erupting volcano, Vesuvius.

Authoritative as it sounded, this explanation still failed to satisfy everyone. Wilton Marion Krogman, Professor of Physical Anthropology at the University of Pennsylvania, came across the Reeser case in the Florida newspapers while on holiday in 1951 and was fascinated. But his interest was more professional than most – Professor Krogman was a world-renowned expert on the identification of human bones and had conducted ground-breaking research on the effect of fire on the human body. In his opinion, Dr Snyder's burning-fat theory was at best an educated guess and was far from a scientific explanation.

Professor Krogman initially laid out his objections to the official explanation of Mary Reeser's death in an article for *Pageant* magazine (October 1952) and later (in 1964), published an in-depth study in *The General Medical and Historical Chronicle*. He began by objecting to the notion that a person could be incinerated by her own body fat. "The body is over 90 per cent water – perhaps even a higher percentage in very fat people," he wrote. "I find it hard to believe that a human body, once ignited, will literally consume itself. . . . [It will] burn itself out, as does a candlewick, guttering in the last residual pool of melted wax."

Whatever had incinerated Mrs Reeser had vaporized all the water in her body. Professor Krogman did not believe that burning fat – even in large amounts – could achieve this. Indeed, he believed that the melting fat would itself drown the blaze. He went on to cite experiments in which a dead body was burned in a furnace for over twelve hours at a time: "Only at 30,000°F plus (over 16,600°C), have I seen bones fuse – or melt, so that it ran and became volatile. These are very great heats – they would sear, char, scorch, or otherwise mar or effect everything within a considerable radius. What I'm driving at is this – the terrific destruction of Mrs Reeser's body (bones included), must have been accompanied by such heat that the room, itself, should have been burned much more than it was." Yet even the floor beneath the circle of burned carpet and the ceiling above Mrs Reeser's head had remained relatively unharmed. The heat damage to anything below four feet from the floor was minor.

The furnace in the experiments Professor Krogman referred to, needed to be fed with powerful jets of pressured air and large amounts of fuel. On the other hand, normal crematoria operate at much lower temperatures than 30,000°F, and for much less than 12 hours. These furnaces will usually take two or three hours to break down a corpse at 2,000 to 3,000°F (about 1,100–1,600°C). Furnace operators do not, however, aim to reduce the body to the "crisp ash" found in Mrs Reeser's room but settle for a lumpy slag in which the heavier pieces of bone remain solid. (To produce a fine powder – necessary if the ashes are to be scattered – a special grinding machine called a cremulator is used.)

In *Ablaze!* (investigator Larry E. Arnold's thorough examination of the phenomena of bizarre fire deaths), crematorium operator John Grenoble describes cremation with gruesome precision: "As the fire jets heat up, hair on the corpse quickly burns with a blue flame, the head snaps back, and the body tries to actually sit up in the casket. Bones begin to explode at the relatively low temperature of 700–800°F, and the chest cavity might open. Rapidly soaring heat reddens the body, its skin turning black then splitting; the flesh carbonizes, then is oxidized.

"The corpse is typically subjected to 2,200°F (1,200°C) for 90 minutes. Muscles and organs gradually burn from the bones, which continue crackling in innumerable small explosions. The retort's temperature is then lowered to around 1,700°F (900°C) and the bone fragments are cooked for another hour to an hour-and-a-half." This process demands 40 to 45 gallons of fuel oil, powerful air jets and a sealed furnace chamber. None of these were available in Mrs Reeser's apartment.

Krogman went on to cite the stopped clock found in the apartment. Broken by the same heat that cracked the mirror and melted the plastic fittings, its dial showed 4.20 a.m. Since the painters broke down the door just past 8.00 a.m., this allowed around four hours for the cremation. The professor stated that, in his opinion, an unassisted fire could not destroy an adult human body so thoroughly in so short a time.

But Krogman had to admit that many elements in the case baffled him: "When human flesh burns it gives off an acrid, evil-smelling odor, especially if burning free in a room or in the open. How 175 pounds of mortal flesh could burn with no detectable or discernible smoke or odor permeating the whole building – well experience says differently!"

Then there was the victim's shrunken skull – reduced to "the size of an orange." But skulls subjected to great heat do not shrink – they explode just like an over-heated pressure cooker, as this passage from T.E. Lawrence's *Seven Pillars of Wisdom* demonstrates: "[We] went to see [the captured town of Sharkeui], in a penny steamer, with Prince Jamil and a gorgeous staff. The Bulgars, when they came, had massacred the Turks; as they retired, the Bulgar peasants went too. So the Turks found hardly anyone to kill. A greybeard was led on board for the Commander-in-Chief [Enver Pasha] to bait. At last Enver tired of this. He signed two of his bravo aides, and throwing open the furnace door, said, 'Push him in.' The old man screamed, but the officers were stronger and the door was slammed to on his jerking body. We turned, feeling sick, to go away, but Enver, his head on one side, listening, halted us. So we listened till there came a crash within the furnace. He smiled and nodded, saying, 'Their heads always pop like that.' "

Krogman states that "in the presence of heat sufficient to destroy the soft tissues the skull would burst – explode, literally – into many pieces. I have experimented on this, using cadaver heads, and can but say I've never known an exception to this rule." Yet whatever had incinerated Mrs Reeser had released the boiling fluids in her skull without bursting it.

Summing up the strange circumstances of Mrs Reeser's death, Professor Krogman pointed out that many similar mysterious deaths by fire have been recorded, but that "conventional" science had yet to seriously address them. In fact, said Krogman, Mary Reeser was a victim of a bizarre and, fortunately, rare accident known as Spontaneous Human Combustion, shortened to SHC. All the evidence would suggest that this is due to internal fires – that is, burning that begins inside the victim's body and works its way outward. Having listed a number of cases that sounded strikingly similar to Mary Reeser's, Professor Krogman concluded, with a kind of exasperated perplexity: "Here then is a monotonously consistent pattern which almost gives the lie to mere coincidence. Such things can't happen! But they seemed to have happened – again and again and again!''

It was probably Krogman's eminence as an expert in death by fire that led him to stick out his neck this far. Although in the past both medical practitioners and the law courts have accepted SHC as a fact, over the last 100 years it has generally been rejected as a ridiculous superstition.

Researchers into possible SHC cases are often faced with the sheer dogmatism of the skeptics, which recalls Ring Lardner's classic line, '' 'Shut up' he explained.'' Yet it has to be admitted that this attitude sounds totally logical. Fires need oxygen, otherwise they go out. And there is simply not enough free oxygen in the human body to start, let alone maintain, a blaze. Since our insides contain no combustible material – on the contrary, they are full of fire retardant liquid – no natural process could ignite so much as a spark. In fact, SHC sounds as improbable as a bucket of water bursting into flames.

But then, science has been wrong before – with considerable frequency. It has always showed a ferocious resistance to what are called "paradigm shifts" – basic changes of viewpoint, such as the recognition that the earth goes round the sun. In his book *Life on Mars*, the astronomer Fred Hoyle points out that when paradigm shifts occur, the scientists who were wrong like to pretend that their past record is nonexistent. And he adds that this process is currently taking place in the eminent scientific journal *Nature*, "a publication with an unhappy record on this subject, with a history extending back beyond modern times to the first editions of that magazine in 1869–70."

But the history of scientific stupidity extends back long before that and occasionally includes men of genius. On September 13, 1768, French peasants in the fields near Luce heard a violent crash like a thunderclap and saw a great stone object hurtle down from the sky. The French Academy of Sciences asked the great chemist Lavoisier for a report, but he was convinced that stones did not fall out of the sky and told them that all the witnesses must be mistaken or lying. It was not until the nineteenth century that the Academy finally accepted the reality of meteorites. Again, in the early days of steam locomotion, Dr Dionysius Lardner (1793–1859), Professor of Natural Philosophy (physics) and Astronomy at London's University College, announced that highspeed rail travel would never come about as the passengers on a speeding train would be unable to breathe and would asphyxiate. Other medical authorities believed that sheer speed would stop the heart.

Yet even scientists learn from experience. In 1943, Lieutenant Grimai Cox of the Indian Army, showed the naturalist Dr John Cloudsley-Thomas his arm which was covered with circular, one-and-a-quarter-inch scars. He explained that in March 1941, while drifting in a lifeboat in the south Atlantic, he and his crew had been attacked by a 20-foot giant squid. The monster had lacerated his arm with the serrated suckers and dragged another man overboard. Cox half-expected the scientist to call him a liar but Cloudsley-Thomas merely expressed amazement that an *Architeuthis Longimanus* (or southern giant squid) "that small" had managed to drag a man overboard. A century earlier, giant squids were regarded as mythical, but since that time science had established the existence of squids measuring up to and over 60 feet long.

The progress of Spontaneous Combustion from myth to scientific fact has been painfully slow and by no means inevitable. It was known and accepted in the early nineteenth century. Captain Marryat used it in his early novel *Jacob Faithful*, in which the hero's mother dies by Spontaneous Combustion in the first chapter. Jacob is the son of a man who lives on a boat on the River Thames, and both his father and mother are heavy consumers of gin – his mother is also grotesquely fat. One night, smoke issues from their cabin and the father staggers out and jumps overboard. Black smoke billows from the open door and when Jacob fights his way in, his mother has turned into "a sort of unctuous cinder" in the center of the bed. Jacob goes on to explain that she perished from Spontaneous Combustion, "an inflammation of the gases generated from the spirits absorbed into the system." Marryat is correct in that many victims of Spontaneous Combustion are overweight and addicted to liquor, but almost certainly wrong about the alcoholic gases catching fire. (Mrs Reeser, for example, was only known to drink beer, and that on rare occasions.)

Almost two decades later, Dickens used Spontaneous Combustion to get rid of one of the characters in *Bleak House*, the drunken rag and bone dealer Krook. As we will see in chapter 3, the renowned author was shocked by the negative reaction the scene generated in scientific circles. The case for and against Spontaneous Combustion was strongly debated in England for a few months in 1853, and Dickens seems to have won the argument. Yet, 70 years later, in Arthur L. Hayward's *The Dickens Encyclopaedia*, the author ends his account of Mr Krook with the words, "The possibility of Spontaneous Combustion in human beings has been finally disproved."

And the 1955 edition of *Forensic Medicine* by Smith and Fiddes, a textbook for students and practitioners, covers the subject of SHC with the following entry: "Spontaneous Combustion of the human body cannot occur, and no good purpose can be served by discussing it."

Clearly human prejudice, even in the face of irrefutable evidence, is virtually ineradicable.

2

The Anger of the Gods

Spontaneous Human Combustion must have been happening throughout history. But we have no early records of it – presumably because our ancestors thought that people who turned to a pile of ashes had incurred the anger of the gods and been struck by a thunderbolt. When Jenny Randles and Peter Hough studied historical records for their book Spontaneous Human Combustion, *they decided that the earliest authentically-recorded case to meet their criteria came as late as 1613.*

On June 26 that year, carpenter John Hitchen of Christchurch, England, went to the bed he shared with his wife and child. Hitchen's mother-in-law, Agnes Russell, slept in a separate bed in the same room. In the night, the old woman was woken by what felt to be a violent blow to her cheek. Sitting up in the dark she cried out for help, but an electrical storm was raging and nobody seemed to hear her. Eventually, Mrs Russell made her way to her son-in-law's bed and realized to her horror that it was surrounded by smoke. She shook her daughter awake and between them they managed to drag John Hitchen's smouldering body outside the house, but it was clearly too late for both him and the child.

Hitchen's corpse became too hot to approach as it continued to burn from the inside – although smoke poured from his orifices, there was initially no outward sign of fire damage. John Hilliard, a local clergyman, noted in his 1613 pamphlet *Fire From Heaven*, that the body "was consumed to ashes, and no fire seene, lying there-in smoking and smothering three days and three nights, not to be quenched by water, nor the help of man's hand."

One final oddity – the bereaved Mrs Hitchen discovered that the side of her body nearest to the blaze victim's had suffered burns, yet she had not wakened until her mother shook her. This seems inexplicable. Surely a person whose flesh was burning would wake up immediately? It seems equally odd that John Hitchen took three days to stop smouldering and that the fire had apparently started inside him.

We also note that a storm was raging with thunder and lightning. Fireballs are often produced by storms – those curious globes of plasma that can pass through walls and may cause tremendous damage when they explode – yet which paradoxically give off no heat. Is it conceivable that the "fire" that consumed John Hitchen was not the normal variety, but some unknown force of nature connected with plasma – a highly charged gas made of ions, atoms stripped of their outer electrons?

Sixty years after the Hitchen case, Professor Mathiaeus Jacobeus in his *Collection Academique*, described a similar fire death in Paris. In this case, an impoverished alcoholic woman sat down to sleep on a pallet of straw but during the night she was "consumed along with her chair by an internal fire" – again, this "internal" element. Investigators sifted the ashes but "only her skull and extreme joints of her fingers were found; all the rest was reduced to cinders."

In his book *Ablaze!*, SHC researcher Larry Arnold cites another French account from the seventeenth century of death by "internal fire." This quotation comes from Thomas H. Bartholini's 1654 pamphlet, *Historia Anatomicarum Rariorum*: "To stir up a fire in the belly from excessive inhaling of wine spirits is foreign neither to reason nor experience. Doctors from Lyon . . . . studying the corpse of a certain woman to determine the cause of death, report that an enormous flame, filling the entire abdominal cavity all around, burst forth but was quickly extinguished. . . . The cause of the flame was believed [to be] wine often swallowed by that woman. . . ."

Bartholini goes on to cite an earlier case of SHC. In this one "a knight [called] Polonus, during the time of good queen Bona Sforza [who reigned in Milan from 1469–1476], consumed two ladles of strong wine, vomited a flame and was thereupon totally consumed, according to a report from his parents, Mr and Mrs Eberhard Vortius."

John Henry Cohausen also mentions this case in a Dutch medical text published in 1717. At the time of writing, the death of this fifteenth-century knight appears to be the first documented case of Spontaneous Human Combustion – others almost certainly predate it, but have yet to be unearthed.

The two cases Bartholini cites are different in one basic essential – the knight was alive as he burned, while the woman was dead and combusted during an autopsy – yet he believed that the cause of both the fires was linked to the victims' drinking. In the case of the unnamed woman, the pamphlet goes on to state that before her death she had heavily imbibed "hot Theriacus water," a strongly-alcoholic beverage used to cure snakebite. The "strong wine" drunk by Sir Polonus was another name for brandy (often called burnt wine or brent wine), one of the few spirits available in medieval Europe.

Theodoric the Great (454–526 AD), was an Ostrogoth emperor who ruled Italy for 33 prosperous years and cemented a peaceful relationship between Rome and the Gothic tribes to the north of the Alps. Unfortunately, he himself was said to suffer from a bizarre malady – his skin would spontaneously catch fire if anybody rubbed him. It is possible that his body harbored some odd chemical property but it is now beyond investigation. Theodoric's tomb still survives in Ravenna, Italy, but his bones were scattered when it was converted into the church of Santa Maria della Rotunda.

Alcohol was also the suspected cause in the next recorded case of SHC – which is also one of those mentioned by Dickens in the preface to *Bleak House*. At around 8.00 p.m. on February 19, 1725, Jean Millet, innkeeper of the Lion d'Or in Rheims, retired to bed with his wife Nicole. A few hours later Mme Millet got out of bed complaining of the cold and went down to the kitchen to sit by the fire. Jean Millet later testified that this was a fairly normal occurrence, since his wife was an alcoholic and would often sit drinking by the fire into the small hours.

At about 2.00 a.m., Jean Millet was awakened again, this time by the smell of smoke. Bellowing "Fire!", the innkeeper roused his guests and hurried to the kitchen. Fortunately, for science, an apprentice surgeon called Claude-Nicolas Le Cat was staying at the Lion d'Or and carefully recorded the scene by the hearth: "The woman was found consumed on February 20, 1725, at a distance of a foot-and-a-half from the hearth in her kitchen. A part of the head only, with a portion of the lower extremities and a few of the vertebrae, had escaped combustion. A foot-and-a-half of the flooring under the body had been consumed, but a kneading-trough and a powder tub, which were very near the body, had sustained no injury. M. Chretien, a surgeon, examined the remains of the body with every judicial formality."

Jean Millet was immediately arrested on suspicion of murdering his wife. At his trial, the prosecution claimed that the late Mme Millet had been a shrewish, drunken woman and that Jean had decided to do away with her when he became enamored of one of the serving wenches. Why and how he had managed to completely incinerate the body was left unexplained. Millet was nevertheless found guilty.

The case went to appeal and the young Dr Le Cat offered evidence for the defence. In his opinion, Nicole Millet had died "by the visitation of God." By this, he explained, he did not mean that the deity had literally taken a direct hand in the matter but that, by ill luck, the alcohol in the woman's belly had somehow caught fire and reduced her to ashes. This time the court decided Millet was innocent and he was released. Unfortunately, his health and business were ruined and he died shortly thereafter. Nevertheless, Dr Le Cat believed that a blow had been struck for both justice and science because the High Court judges had brought in the first legal verdict of "death by Spontaneous Combustion."

The opinion that alcoholism could cause Spontaneous Human Combustion was popular among eighteenth-century medical practitioners, as well as the clergy. Doctors reasoned that since alcohol vapor burns, heavy drinkers must be in danger of exploding into flame. The reasoning of the clergy was equally simple – they regarded it as self-evident that the fires of Spontaneous Combustion and the fires of hell were identical and that SHC was therefore clear evidence of God's justice in action.

For upper class drinkers, who accepted the widespread notion that Spontaneous Combustion only happened among the poor, the death of Countess Cornelia of Zangaria and Bandi must have come as a shock.

In 1731, the 62-year-old Countess Bandi was in residence at her mansion at Cesina, in central Italy. After dinner on the night of March 14, she complained of feeling a "dull and heavy" drowsiness and retired early. She did not fall asleep immediately, but spent several hours lying in bed, talking and praying with her maidservant. Eventually, the Countess dozed off and the maid closed the bed curtains and crept out.

In his book *Dissertazione Epistolare Istorico-Filosofica*, Father Giuseppe Bianchini described the scene the maids found the following morning. The room, he said, was filled with smoke. The bed was not occupied and no sign of the Countess could, at first, be seen. Then, on the floor, four feet from the bed, they saw "a heap of ashes, two legs untouched from the foot to the knee, with their stockings on; between them was the lady's head, whose brains, half of the back part of the skull, and the whole chin, were burned to ashes, among which were found three fingers, blackened; all the rest was ashes, which had this particular quality, that they left in the hand, when taken up, a greasy and stinking moisture."

Every surface in the room was covered with a "moist and ash colored soot" but, other than the incinerated Countess, there was no sign of fire damage. The soot "hung on the walls, moveables, and utensils" and "penetrated into the chest of drawers even to foul the linens." Candleholders were found to contain nothing but wicks, the tallow having melted and run away (just as would be found 220 years later in Mary Reeser's apartment). A lamp was found standing on the floor but this was empty of oil and did not appear to have been involved in the death. In the room above the Countess's death chamber, Bianchini noted "that from the lower part of the windows trickled down a greasy, loathsome, yellowish liquor," which gave off a nauseating odor.

Studying the case 14 years later, Paul Rolli of the British Royal Society could only suggest that Countess Bandi had been struck by lightning. Witnesses, however, insisted that there had been no storm over Cesina that night and, furthermore, the sound of a lightning strike would have roused the whole household.

Father Bianchini could offer no explanation himself, but believed that the victim had "burned to ashes while standing, as her skull was fallen perpendicular between her legs; and that the back-part of her head had been damaged more than the fore-part was." This seems to suggest either that the Countess had slumped in a sitting position to burn, or that she had been consumed in an instant before she could fall flat on the floor.

To further contradict the generally held view, it seemed that the Countess was not a heavy drinker; but the Marquis Scipio Maffei, official investigator of the death, noted that it was rumored in the town that the Countess "was accustomed to bathe all her body in camphorated spirit of wine [brandy]." Maffei wrote in the *Journal de Medecine* (vol. 26) that "the use of this drug is one of the causes of this phenomenon." This is clearly unlikely. A thin layer of burning alcohol, even if the victim had only just bathed in it, would have done little more than blacken and blister the skin.

Another suspected cause of the blaze, at least among the peasantry, was witchcraft. Italy had, and still has, a rich folklore concerning witches and their nocturnal activities. In the eighteenth century it was common to blame unexplained deaths on witches. Others suspected that the Countess herself might have been involved in black magic.

An element of witchcraft was also suspected in a British case of 1744. In that year, 60-year-old Grace

Heidi Whittock-Knott with a charred table that burnt mysteriously in her home in Somerset, England

Pett was living in the port of Ipswich, in Suffolk. Grace was a local fisherman's wife and her family is described in the local parish records as "poor." One of her few extravagances was her tobacco pipe, and she would often sit puffing on it beside the kitchen fire in the early hours of the morning. *The Philosophical Transactions of the Royal Society of Great Britain* (1744–45), gives the following description of her death: "On the night of April 9, 1744, she got up from bed as usual. Her daughter, who slept with her, did not perceive she was absent till the next morning when she awoke. Soon after which she put on her clothes, and going down to the kitchen, found her mother stretched out on the right side, with her head near the grate; the body extended on the hearth, with legs on the floor, which was of deal [rough pine], having the appearance of a log of wood, consumed by a fire without apparent flame.

"On beholding the spectacle, the girl ran in great haste and poured over her mother's body some water contained in two large vessels in order to extinguish the fire; while the fetid odor and smoke which exhaled from the body almost suffocated some of the neighbors who had hastened to the girl's assistance. The trunk was in some measure incinerated and resembled a heap of coals covered with ashes. The head, the arms, the legs, and the thighs had also participated in the burning."

Certain curious aspects of the case aroused special interest in the Royal Society. For example, until water was poured on the burning woman, little or no smell was said to have come from the burnt remains. At the time, several other people lived in the house, including the victim's daughter, but no one smelt a fire until the body was actually discovered. Most of Grace's corpse had already been reduced to ashes, so at least two gallons of body fluid must also have been vaporized. Yet no one in the house had noticed anything.

The source of fire was also a mystery. Grace was found lying with her head near the grate of the fireplace, but this was irrelevant since the fire was not lit. For want of any better conjecture, it was suggested that Grace's clothes had been set alight by her own pipe, but it was hard to see quite how it could have happened since she had only been wearing a linen shift and stockings – hardly enough to incinerate her. In addition to which, the greatest destruction seems to have centered around her torso – the area of a body that is least likely to be damaged by fire due to its high liquid content.

A Mr R. Love attended the coroner's inquest into the death of Grace Pett, and sent the Royal Society the following description of the remains: "Ye feet and lower part of ye Leggs were not burnt . . . . ye Stockings on ye parts remaining, not Singed; very little of ye parts of ye Leggs yt burnt lay on ye wood floor the rest of ye body on a Brick hearth in ye Chimney; part of the head not burnt a Body of ffire in her breast in ye morning, which was Quenched with water, her bone chiefly calcined and ye whole so farr reduced to ashes as to be put in ye Coffin with a shovel. . . ."

It is notable that Mr Love maintained the "body of ffire" (the main area affected by the fire) to be the victim's chest. The Society's own report described Grace's body as being reduced by a "fire without apparent flame." Both descriptions recall the case of the Christchurch carpenter John Hitchen, whose corpse burned internally for three days.

As with Nicole Millet, Countess Bandi and Mary Reeser, the blaze that destroyed Grace Pett did virtually no damage to the immediate surroundings. The Royal Society reported that lying near her body were "the clothes of a child and a paper screen, which had sustained no injury from the fire." The stockings on the undamaged part of the legs were "not Singed," according to Mr Love's report, and the pine boards beneath the corpse were said by the daughter to be "neither singed or discolor'd." The only damage to the brick fireplace was a deposit of melted human fat that had sunk in so deep "as not to be scoured out."

The coroner set the approximate time of death as between 10.00 p.m. and 6.00 a.m. on the grounds that nobody had seen or heard Mrs Pett die. But 55 years later, in 1799, someone calling himself Mr B wrote to the *Ipswich Magazine*, reporting "that some ship carpenters going to work about five o'clock in the morning, saw a great light in the room, broke into it, and found her in a blaze: they then procured some bowls of water from a pump which was near the door, in the street; on throwing it on the body it made the same hssing [sic] as if thrown on red-hot iron," Failing to douse the blaze, the men hurried away.

If Mr B's story was true, then the events of that morning sound like a cross between a horror movie and a Keystone Cops comedy. But on the whole, it sounds like the folklore that springs up long after such an event. For it fails to answer the obvious questions –

why did the fire fighters not arouse the household and why did they not appear at the coroner's court?

The Royal Society account reaches no firm conclusion, but notes that Mrs Pett was said to have been drinking the evening before, implying that she was yet another alcoholic who had gone up in flames. The coroner did not agree. Mr Love reported that she was "not in liquor [when she died] nor addicted to drink Gin."

There the matter rested until recently. In the 1980s, researcher Peter Christie began to look into the death of Grace Pett and discovered an eerie, supernatural side to the story. Reading the comments made by Mr B in the *Ipswich Magazine* in 1799, Christie came across another report by somebody who signed himself "J.S.". This correspondent claimed that Grace Pett was well-known in the town as a practising witch, and that one of her own curses had backfired and killed her. It seemed that a local farmer called Garnham had been losing sheep to some unknown disease. Believing that they might have been hexed, he consulted a "magician" called Mr White, and was told that the only way to break the spell was to take one of the sick sheep and burn it alive. Garnham refused to do this but his wife decided it was worth a try.

Ordering a farmhand to bind one of the sick animals, the farmer's wife had it dropped on a blazing hearth. The terrified animal tried to leap out of the flames when the bandages binding its legs burned through, but it was skewered with a pitchfork and thrown back. (It should be remembered that our own humanitarian attitudes were unknown in the eighteenth century –

it is recorded that the Parisians of that period enjoyed throwing live cats or dogs out of high windows and that everyone found it irresistibly amusing to see them burst on the cobbles.)

According to J.S., the sheep was incinerated on the same night Grace Pett burned to ashes. (In *The Golden Bough*, Sir James Frazer mentions the belief that curses can be reflected back on the sorcerer who invokes them. This can be found in cultures all over the world.) Peter Christie also came across a book, published in 1875, called *Grace Pett: A Tale of Witchcraft* by Elisabeth Cotton in which the latter claims that the night Grace Pett died, Farmer Garnham's sheep all recovered.

In the first half of the eighteenth century, most recorded deaths from Spontaneous Combustion were in England, France and Italy, although some of the strangest occurred in France. In 1749, in the town of Plerquer, 80-year-old Madame de Boiseon was huddled by the fire, fending off the February cold, when her maid left the room for a short time. When the girl returned, Mme de Boiseon was sheathed in flame and was apparently quite dead. The frantic maid tried to beat out the flames with her hands, but soon gave up as her own skin caught fire. She then tried pouring water on her mistress but, strangely enough, this only seemed to make the fire worse. The blaze eventually extinguished itself, but not until Mme de Boiseon had been reduced to ashes. The fire was said to have passed from her midriff out to her extremities, slowly destroying both flesh and bones, the same way a rag doll might smoulder. The case suggests that the "fire" was some kind of unknown chemical reaction that consumed flesh.

The case was reported to Claude-Nicolas Le Cat (who had remained interested in SHC since defending Jean Millet on a charge of murdering his wife), by a priest named Father Boineau, who also mentioned that Mme de Boiseon was reputed to be a heavy drinker. So, it seems, was another unnamed victim of Spontaneous Combustion reported by Le Cat, who died in the same month "under circumstances very similar," in Dinan in northwestern France.

No reports of SHC-like deaths have come to light during the next 20-year period. Then, on New Year's Eve in 1770, the first reported case occurred in America. Hannah Bradshaw was about 30 years old and lived on an upper floor of a house on Division Street, New York. Described as a "large and robust woman," Hannah was known to be a heavy imbiber and, on that particular holiday, was described by acquaintances as having "drunk a little too freely."

Hannah apparently went home before midnight and so missed seeing in the New Year. The next morning a maid arrived early, but in view of the season was unsurprised to find the door bolted and to receive no answer when she knocked. By 11.00 a.m. she was sufficiently concerned to ask the downstairs tenant to crawl through Hannah's window to see if she had been incapacitated by anything worse than a hangover.

The window seemed to have been covered or painted over, so the neighbor could not see inside. On forcing an entry, he was shocked to find the room full of smoke and apparently deserted. Then, behind a screen, he saw what was left of Hannah Bradshaw. . . . A contemporary account states that "the flesh was entirely burnt off the bones of the whole body and limbs, except a small part of the skull, a little on one of the shoulders, the lower part of the right leg and foot . . . . and left [foot] lying on the floor; stocking burnt as far as the leg and no further." The remaining bones were calcined and "crumbled to dust between the fingers."

Hannah's incineration had made a four-foot hole through the floorboards and a joist beneath was "burnt almost through." The heat of her death had sweated turpentine from the oak wainscoting. The ceiling, walls and window were covered in a sticky soot which made them "as black as if covered in lamp black." It was also noted that the ceiling above the victim was, as in the case of Mary Reeser, unburned – apparently contradicting the universal rule that the greatest amount of heat from a fire travels upward. The screen was undamaged, while a nearby chair leg and seat were only burned "as they were in the compass of the hole in the floor and no further."

This account, which appeared in *The New York Journal and General Advertiser*, concluded: "It is extremely surprising that with such an intense degree of heat as was necessary to consume the floor, etc., with the body and to calcine the bones, the fire should have stopped of itself without burning the house, or even scorching the screen – which is hardly conceivable if the fire had blazed. And if it did not, it is equally inconceivable that the heat should have been so intense."

In *Historia Ecclesiastica de Saxonia* (1482), Professor Albert Krantz described a burning pestilence that swept the army of Godfrey of Bulloigne in central France, during 1099 AD. "Men burned," he said, "being touched with an invisible fire, that pierced into the very bowels and vitals, by occasion of which, the hands of some, and feet of others, fell off." Ten years before, in 1089, a similar malady had struck the people in the French region of Lorraine. Marcellus Donatus wrote in *De Medica Historia Mirabili Libri Sex* (1586), that the victims suffered the "burning of an invisible fire in their entrails and . . . . some cut off a hand or a foot when the burning began, that it should go no further."

Were Marcellus Donatus and Professor Krantz simply using fanciful language to describe a plague of leprosy, or were these mass attacks of Spontaneous Human Combustion?

It was also noted that, because the fire had burned clean into the lower room, it "could not have stopped for want of air." This point will be worth remembering when we come to consider recent attempts to explain SHC.

On March 2, 1773, the curse of SHC returned across the Atlantic to kill 52-year-old Mary Clues in Coventry, England. At around 5.30 a.m., neighbors saw that smoke was belching from the windows of Mary's Gosford Street home and they broke in. They found her remains stretched between the fireplace and her bed. Her arms, hands, neck and torso had been reduced to ash and brittle, shattered bone. Only her legs and fleshless backbone and skull remained in one piece. Although lying within a couple of feet of the highly flammable feather bed, the fire had not spread and the bedding was undamaged.

At the time of her death, Mary Clues had been ill with jaundice (among other things), and her habit of drinking "at least half a pint of rum or aniseed water" a day may have undermined her health. Dr Wilmer, who was called to the death scene, believed that alcohol was the likely cause of the combustion, but a neighbor remembered that Mary had recently sworn that the Devil had appeared to her in her bedroom and threatened to take her away with him.

There were also rumors of diabolical intervention in the case of Don Gio Maria Bertholi. During October 1776, the priest was visiting the house of his brother-in-law at Fenile, Italy. He had retired to his room to pray, but just moments later the sound of screams and flailing came from the chamber. Rescuers burst in and found Don Bertholi bathed in blue fire across the upper half of his body. Strangely, it was reported that flames receded of their own accord as helpers moved closer, then went out altogether.

The priest, in great pain, told of how a "sharp blow" had struck his right hand, then his shirt had erupted into flame. This garment (apart from the cuffs) was totally destroyed but the sackcloth vest he wore underneath was quite unharmed. Bertholi's cap had burned on his head but his hair was unsinged.

During the next few hours, the priest's skin separated from his upper body and hung in shreds. The nails of his left hand – not the one that had received the "sharp blow" – also became detached. Although complaining only of great thirst, Don Bertholi was clearly in agony and survived just four days. To the end, he insisted that there had been no fire source in the room before he had started to burn and investigators found this to be true.

In 1779, France once again suffered two apparent cases of SHC within 12 months. In February, Mary Ann Jauffret, the alcoholic widow of a shoemaker, was consumed while sitting in a chair at her supper-table. A surgeon called Roccus attended the scene and reported that just part of her skull, one foot and a hand had survived the incineration. Other than that, Mme Jauffret (and the chair), had been reduced to ash and calcined bone. The table and other nearby objects were unharmed.

It is worth noting that Mme Jauffret was what the eighteenth-century medical profession believed to be a typical SHC victim – female, old, overweight and alcoholic. And although cases like that of Don Bertholi are an exception to the rule, it has to be admitted that, as a simple matter of statistics, people in these categories do seem to be at a higher risk than the rest of the population.

So far, the cases we have considered involved single individuals. But on December 10, 1779, a Parisian couple named Bias were found together in their smoke-filled, but otherwise unharmed, house. The upper halves of their bodies had been reduced to a mass of charcoal. The medical report on the tragedy noted that the head of one of the victims was bloated and puffed-up. Only a nearby chair and table showed any heat damage, and neighbors claimed that they had heard Mme Bias talking and moving about only two hours before the corpses were discovered.

Here again, the circumstances seem to be offering some clue to the nature of Spontaneous Combustion. It is possible, but unlikely, that the two burst into flames simultaneously. The circumstances suggest that they were laying asleep when one of them began to burn and that neither of them noticed what was happening. Whatever strange chemical reaction occurred in one, spread to the other and killed them as they lay together.

The following year, in Caen in northern France, a 60-year-old spinster was found reduced to ash in her apartment. The attending surgeon, Louis Valentin, reported that only her feet and skull had remained solid while the rest of her body had been reduced to ash. The whole room was coated in a greasy soot. There was a fire in the room's grate but the woman had died some distance from it. Valentin added that the woman was known to enjoy "strong liquors and petting animals," although what bearing he thought the latter point may have had on the case is unclear.

Two years later, in 1782, a woman called Thuars died in the same town. A sexagenarian spinster, Mlle Thuars was described as "exceedingly corpulent" and was also an alcoholic. Investigators found that only her feet and seven bones remained identifiable as human. The rest was ash and calcined bone fragments that "became dust by the least pressure." Once again, there was minimal fire damage to the room.

The survival of bodily extremities, such as hands, feet, and skulls is another typical factor in Spontaneous Human Combustion. The skulls are often partially calcined and the flesh is partly or completely burnt away. Hands and forearms seem to survive if the arms are spread out and not in contact with the torso. Feet and lower legs often survive totally unmarked, separated neatly from the rest of the remains as if severed by an axe. The lack of damage is obviously one of the most puzzling aspects of SHC – stockings may not even be singed. Since the degree of heat necessary to incinerate a human torso should roast any flesh within meters, it would seem to follow that SHC may involve less heat than might be supposed.

This could also explain why some of the victims seem to have failed to notice it. In England, in 1788, a gentleman entered a room in which his chambermaid was scrubbing the floor and was horrified to notice that her back was on fire. Incredibly, she seemed quite unaware of her danger. Her master tried to smother the fire but the woman died before it could be extinguished.

This again seems odd. A normal fire can be put out fairly quickly by starving it of air. This is not true of a chemical reaction. If iron filings and sulphur are mixed together, then subjected even to a small degree of heat, a reaction begins that soon converts it to a bubbling brown liquid. Even though the heat is removed, it will continue to bubble until it is converted to a solid mass of iron sulphide. Could some similar reaction take place in Spontaneous Combustion?

It would certainly seem that there are two categories of SHC. One seems to begin inside the body (somewhere in the region of the solar plexus), and spreads outwards, while the other – like that of the maid scrubbing the floor or Don Bertholi – starts outside the body, usually on the upper half. In cases of the latter type, it seems possible – as Dr Lemoyne Snyder suggested in the Mary Reeser case – that the "fuel" is the layer of fat immediately beneath the human skin. Such an explanation might certainly explain why Don Bertholi's skin became detached from his body after he was burned – the anchoring layer of fat had literally gone. We will look more closely at this theory in a later chapter.

In 1796, the painter John Constable noted on a sketch of a house in the village of Capel, near Ipswich: "Curious circumstances happened in this cottage a few years since, a poor woman being burnt entirely to ashes." Unfortunately, the rest of the note is now illegible so no further details can be extracted about this death.

A month before the dawn of the new century, on December 10, 1799, France suffered yet another case of near-total incineration. Again, the victim was a Madame Bias, wife of the police inspector of Pont Neuf, who was found so completely burned that her "whole trunk was a mass of carbon" and her "sex was no longer distinguishable." Monsieur Neveux, the region's health officer, reported that, of the whole corpse, only one foot was left "with its natural color." Neighbors claimed to have spoken with Mme Bias only two hours before she was found.

Oddly enough, the Pont Neuf case was a double coincidence – not only was the victim called Bias (as in the Paris case of 1779), but both cases took place in France on December 10 in the last year of a decade!

As we have seen, many eighteenth-century doctors accepted Spontaneous Combustion as a fact. Yet, as the Age of Reason advanced and chemical and biological processes became more fully understood, the sheer impossibility of the Spontaneous Combustion of a living creature – made almost entirely of water – began to erode this acceptance. As the nineteenth century progressed, natural philosophers (who were soon beginning to refer to themselves by the newly coined word "scientist") became increasingly skeptical about SHC. It seems odd that skepticism should be regarded as more "scientific" than belief when common sense would suggest that it would be more sensible to keep an open mind and study the facts to decide whether they are true or false. But nineteenth-century science felt that disbelief was less effort, with the result that by 1900 Spontaneous Human Combustion was regarded as an outrageous superstition – a view still held by the majority of scientists today.

It may seem odd that, in spite of the number of authorities who declare it impossible, the public's belief in Spontaneous Combustion has remained as widespread as ever. This may, of course, be merely because we are all fascinated by a gruesome story. But a likelier explanation is that it is because cases of Spontaneous Human Combustion continue to occur.

3

The Inferno of the Demon Drink

1808 was a watershed in the annals of Spontaneous Human Combustion because that was the year of the first scientific analysis of the subject. Pierre-Aime Lair, a respected French scholar, published an article in the Journal de Physique *entitled* On the Combustion of the Human Body, Produced by the Long and Immoderate Use of Spirituous Liquors.

Although Lair's essay was written nearly two centuries ago, we cannot afford to be patronizing – for the truth is that we know just as little as he did. Lair was faced with a simple and obvious problem – how can a human body, which is composed mostly of water, shrivel away like a matchstick left on the hot plate of a stove? Considering that all he had to go on was a mere 20 cases, he managed to acquit himself admirably.

Lair's conclusions were as follows:

1. The victims were invariably long-term alcoholics, prone to imbibe "spirituous liquors" (i.e. brandy).
2. Only women were affected.
3. The victims were all in their latter years.
4. Despite popular opinion, the fires were not ignited spontaneously or internally but came from

some outside source (i.e. a candle, fireplace, lamp or tobacco pipe).

5. Extremities, such as hands and feet, often survived the blaze.
6. Water, when cast on to burning victims, often had no effect or, indeed, made the blaze worse.
7. The heat often did little, or no, damage to combustible items on or near the victim.
8. The combustion of the victim left a residue of melted fat and odorous, greasy ashes as well as a foul smelling and penetrating soot.

Most of the first four points were, as we have seen, rather doubtful. Men, as well as women, have suffered Spontaneous Combustion and we are pretty certain that most of the fires do not start from an outside source. Lair was simply making the common mistake of supposing that Spontaneous Combustion was like ordinary burning. But as we go down his list, it is hard to see how he made this mistake since he also recognized that water has little effect on the burning flesh, which shows fairly clearly that something has happened to the flesh which causes it to blaze and disintegrate – rather as a match head blazes when it is struck.

An American medical journal of 1802 came closer to the truth when it described the death of a Massachusetts grandmother as "rapid disorganization of the human body." But at least Lair's treatise brought Spontaneous Combustion into the arena of scientific debate – an important achievement when France was virtually the Spontaneous Combustion capital of Europe: out of 28 recorded cases, 16 had taken place in France.

It was beginning to spread however. In the year after Lair's treatise, Dr James Apjohn, Professor of Chemistry at the Royal College of Surgeons in Dublin, reported Ireland's first recorded case – a Mrs Peacock (or Pococke) who had died in the Five Pounds Alms House in Limerick sometime during 1780.

Early one morning, the landlord of the alms house, a Mr O'Neill, was awakened by a hysterical guest who babbled that something on fire had just fallen into his room. The pair rushed to the chamber and found a large, smoking hole in the wooden boards of the ceiling. Beneath the hole, on the floor, were the charred remains of Mrs Peacock, heated "as red as copper." No source of fire could be detected in the lady's room – the grate contained only ashes and there were no candles. Furthermore, reported Dr Apjohn, "nothing had caught fire but that part of the floor through which the wretched woman had fallen. Even a small basket made of twigs and a small trunk of dry wood, which lay near the hole, escaped – they were not so much as touched by the fire."

Ireland, up to 1808, had apparently remained free of such cases – or no one bothered to record them. Then matters changed dramatically – no less than three women spontaneously combusted in less than 12 months.

The first case was that of a Mrs Stout of Coote Hill, County Cavan. Her husband failed to notice when she left their bed one night and the next morning found her "burned to a cinder on the floor." The corpse was still smoking but crumbled to dust when he touched it. Weirdly enough, not only were Mrs Stout's surroundings undamaged by the combustion but her "chemise and night-cap escaped uninjured." According to the account given by Dr Apjohn, the woman was known as an "inveterate intoxicator" – meaning not that she intoxicated others but that she was seldom seen sober.

Dr Apjohn also reported on another case of Spontaneous Combustion in Dublin in 1808. Mrs Anne Nelis, aged 45, was found sitting upright in a chair, her torso burned to a cinder. Yet her arms, legs and hair were undamaged. Mrs Nelis, the wife of a wealthy wine importer, had returned rather drunk from a party earlier that night. The scandal attending SHC deaths at that time (due to the belief the combustion was caused by a drunken, debauched lifestyle), led Mr Nelis to pull a few strings and have the matter hushed up. No coroner's inquest was held.

The last apparent SHC death to be reported in Ireland in 1808 took place in County Down, in N. Ireland. The Revd Ferguson reported that a Mrs A.B. – 66-years-old and a known heavy drinker – had died while staying at her brother's house. She and her daughter had retired to their shared bed for several hours when the smell of smoke roused the household. Mrs A.B. was found "as black as coal," but no sign of flame could be seen about her body – to witnesses it appeared that her body was "burning with internal fire." As with other cases of SHC, there was a strange smell in the air and when they tried to move the body it crumbled to lumps of ash and calcined bone.

The strangest aspect of this case was that the woman's daughter was lying beside her in the bed when she combusted. The reason that the younger woman did not immediately awake was explained by the fact that both she and her mother had gone to bed thoroughly drunk. All the same, being unconscious should not have protected her when someone was burning to death right beside her, yet both the daughter and the bedclothes were unharmed.

1811 is also noteworthy in the history of Spontaneous Combustion because that is when Germany had its first recorded SHC case. In the town of Waertefeld, on January 17, a 48-year-old "very intemperate man," Ignatius Meyer, burned to death in his bed. Dr Scherf of Detmold and an eyewitness (Meyer's nephew) reported that the blaze that killed the man had left the bedclothes undamaged.

This odd and baffling feature continues to appear in case after case. An account of the death of an unnamed Englishman in the *Philosophical Magazine* for 1813, states that he was drunk on "tincture of valerian and gum guaiacum," that he had rolled from his bed and "his saturated body burst into flame. The corpse was reduced to a cinder, without materially injuring the bed furniture."

Again in 1816, a French kitchen-maid living 80 miles outside Marseille, was found burned to ash in her room, her arms, head and the rest of the room's contents being undamaged. It is interesting that a M. Pierquin stated in *Reflexions Theorique* that the victim was known to have been in good health and was a non-drinker, contradicting the notion that all SHC victims are alcoholics.

On January 12, 1820, two Frenchwomen died together in the town of Nevers. 90-year-old Mme P. and her elderly servant, both habitual drunkards who shared the same bed, were burned in a fire for which investigators could find "no explanation." Lying in the bed were a pile of ashes, a part of one of Mme P.'s legs (still wearing an undamaged shoe), and the servant's skull. The bed and its curtains were damaged by the twin blaze, but once again the fire had remained localized.

There was a bizarre touch in the case of Mme Thomasse Goret, who burned to ash on New Year's Eve, 1820, in her bedroom in Rouen, France. Her face remained untouched on top of her charred corpse, the fire having (for some reason) ceased as it reached her neck.

So far, one of the problems in trying to understand Spontaneous Combustion was that the victims were usually dead when they were found, or very close to death. Then, in 1822, an interesting exception occurred. An unnamed Italian farmer, 26-years-old, was convinced that he was harboring a blaze in his belly. For a week, the man suffered intermittent fevers and an unpleasant irritation in his stomach. On the seventh day, the symptoms worsened – he indicated that he felt a burning heat ascending from his belly and scorching his throat like "red-hot coals." Those nursing him assumed this was delirium, until his mouth and nose began to smoke. They were shocked to be able to feel the intense heat of the man's breath from two feet away, as if it came from the door of an oven. His thirst was, unsurprisingly, tremendous, but cold water did little to quench it. Eventually, iced water was procured and this, combined with immersion in cold baths, stopped the combustion. It is worth noting also that he displayed a voracious appetite as if he had just come out of a severe fever – a point we shall return to in looking at the relationship between SHC and "hyperthermia," the medical term for the inexplicable superheating of the human body.

There is a second report of an early nineteenth-century survivor that is even more striking. The victim in this case was Professor James Hamilton of the Mathematics faculty of Nashville University, Tennessee. January 5, 1835, was an intensely cold day but the professor braved the temperature and went out for a walk. When he returned home, he lit a fire and then spent about half an hour standing on his porch checking his weather gauges. Suddenly, he felt "a steady pain like a hornet's sting, accompanied by a sensation of heat" on his left thigh. Looking down he was astonished to see "a light flame of the extent of a ten cent piece, having the complexion of pure quicksilver" (liquid mercury). The flame, he said, was two or three inches long and flattened at the top – which suggests that it was burning with considerable vigor, since the flame was jetting out horizontally.

Instinctively, Professor Hamilton swatted at the burning area but it seemed to do no good. It is anyone's guess whether, if he had continued this ineffectual effort, he would have set his hand on fire (as had happened to the maid of Mme Boiseon in 1749). Fortunately, he now tried a more scientific approach. Realizing that flame needs a steady supply of oxygen, Hamilton cupped his hands over the burning area and the fire soon died out. The intense pain continued, however, so Professor Hamilton limped indoors to inspect his leg. With his trousers and long underwear removed, he saw a one-by-three-inch hole gouged obliquely across his lower thigh. Although deep and inflamed, the wound was quite dry and bloodfree.

Examining his clothes, Hamilton found a corresponding hole in his longjohns, but was amazed to see that the wool around the hole was not even scorched. Stranger still, the trousers showed no damage at all despite the fact that Hamilton had distinctly seen the flame emerging from the fabric. All he could find to show that anything odd had happened was a yellowish fuzz on that area of the garment.

John Overton, Professor Hamilton's doctor, inspected the wound and found it odd enough to record the case in the *Transactions of the Medical Society of Tennessee*. The abrasion was painfully deep and took 32 days to heal. Even then, the muscles around the damaged flesh remained sore for a long time and the resulting scar was livid. Hamilton told the doctor that he had lit a small fire half an hour before the strange accident but could not imagine how a spark could have infiltrated his clothes, survived so long and then done so much damage to his leg yet so little to his trousers. Dr Overton, after carefully inspecting the wound, reached the sensible conclusion that the flame was not the result of a spark but of a spontaneous fire starting inside Hamilton's flesh. In his opinion, the professor had suffered "partial human combustion," and if he had not acted with such coolness, he might have been reduced to a pile of ashes like so many others.

The above cases – as well as showing that the

phenomenon need not be fatal – led doctors to conclude that there seem to be two types of Spontaneous Combustion. The Italian farmer with a fire in his belly is typical of internal Spontaneous Human Combustion. Somehow, the victim's entrails start to produce vast amounts of heat and, in most cases, turns them to ash from the middle outwards. On the other hand, Professor Hamilton began to burn as if his leg had turned into a gas jet and his flesh proceeded to burn as easily and rapidly as kindling wood. Doctors decided to call this type "preternatural combustion" (PC).

On the whole, scientists who have taken the trouble to look at the subject have been in favor of preternatural combustion, since it does not necessarily depend on some mysterious form of spontaneous ignition. In the nineteenth century, PC supporters believed that an external heat source, like a dropped pipe, could sometimes set human skin alight. Alcohol in the bloodstream would then greatly increase the chance of combustion and would accelerate the resulting blaze. (It shows how little science has learned about Spontaneous Combustion that the police in the 1951 case of Mary Reeser still thought it might be "preternatural combustion.")

The "demon drink" explanation suffered a setback in 1828. A French researcher called Julia de Fontanelle – a believer in the theory that human preternatural combustion is fuelled by alcohol – published an account of an experiment in the *Revue Medecin Francaise*. Fontanelle described taking strips of meat, saturating them with spirit alcohol and setting them alight. The result was disappointing. Instead of turning to greasy ashes, the

On January 2, 1852, the British Admiralty steam liner *Amazon* set out on her maiden voyage across the Atlantic. The ship was a giant vessel for the period but was already obsolete by technological standards. The Admiralty, with typical bureaucratic conservatism, had refused to utilize the new iron hull designs and had the *Amazon* constructed from timber.

Two days out, sailing with 111 crewmen but only 50 passengers, the *Amazon* suddenly caught fire amidships. The reason for the blaze was never ascertained but the possibility that overheated engine bearings set the wooden hull alight was later suspected. (As the ship was sailing through a storm at the time, an atmospheric electrical discharge like ball lightning was also a possibility.)

Although vast amounts of seawater were pumped on to the fire, it continued to blaze uncontrollably. Eventually Captain Symons was forced to give the order to abandon ship. In the midst of this operation, almost all the lifeboats broke away from their moorings and dropped their human contents into the heaving sea – only 21 out of 161 people survived. The *Amazon* continued to blaze as a sole surviving lifeboat pulled away.

As a result of the *Amazon* fire, iron hulls became a standard feature in all subsequent steamship designs. The risk of combining steel engines with wooden hulls was plainly too great a hazard.

meat roasted on the surface and then the flames died out. Thereupon, Fontanelle poured more alcohol on the meat and relit it with the same result. It was clear that only the alcohol vapor was burning and, while the resulting heat roasted the flesh, it did not actually burn it. In fact, meat can be totally drenched in alcohol but will not burn because the liquid actually protects it. When the flames have drawn out all the alcohol, like the sun evaporating water from a sponge, the meat will burn if held in a steady flame but this hardly proves the case for alcohol fuelled Spontaneous Combustion. Therefore, as often happens when research goes against the tide of scientific opinion, Fontanelle's article was largely ignored.

Meanwhile, as the scientists debated and the preachers sermonized, reports of SHC deaths continued to be recorded. During May 1829, the eminent British surgeon and physician to the King, Dr Thomas Newell, presented a paper in the *Midland Medical and Surgical Reporter* entitled "Observations upon Spontaneous Combustion of the Human Body." Here he reviewed the case of the Mrs Jane Lappiter, a widow in her 60s who had recently died by fire in the English town of Cheltenham. Newell had examined the death scene personally and gave a precise and striking account.

Mrs Lappiter's lodger, Mrs Roper, had last seen her alive at 10.00 p.m. At about 2.30 a.m., Mrs Roper was woken by a loud cracking noise and noticed the smell of smoke. Running to her window, she shouted for assistance and a Mr Overbury responded. He shouldered open Jane Lappiter's bedroom door, from which the smoke was billowing, and looked about for the widow. She was nowhere to be seen. There was only a mass of "slight lurid [glowing] appearance, near the hearth, but not bright enough to enable him to judge, exactly, from what it proceeded."

The influx of fresh air from the open door rekindled

the fire in the "lurid" mass and water had to be fetched to extinguish it. The room was filled with steam and smoke "which had a disagreeable empyreumic [burned meat] smell." Before the air could be cleared, one of the growing crowd of bystanders stumbled on Mrs Lappiter's severed left foot and the authorities were summoned, including Dr Newell. He found the remains of Jane Lappiter lying across the stone hearth in front of the bedroom fireplace. Her right leg was unharmed but her left leg was reduced to ashes down to the ankle. The left foot still wore its shoe and showed "not the least alteration, but was in its natural state." Her abdomen and pelvis "were reduced to ashes, with not a vestige [remaining]." The flesh of her upper abdomen, chest and back was "consumed, leaving the ribs on the right side, and the back bone, without any covering whatever." The ribs themselves had been burnt through, several inches from the vertebrae. Her shoulders, neck and part of her head were also completely incinerated. At her chin, the blaze had taken "an oblique direction, across the face towards the right side of the head, in such a way as to destroy the lower portion of the nose and the right eye." Her left eye and upper nose had, however, "escaped, and were uninjured." The top of her head, her hair and her cotton cap were also quite unburned.

The doctor added that, contrary to the popular preconceptions about Spontaneous Combustion, Jane Lappiter had a thin body and "had scarcely tasted spirits in her time." Friends insisted that she was a virtuous woman who drank only tea and, very occasionally, a small cup of beer. Portions of Mrs Lappiter's petticoats and woollen dress were found unburned within inches of her corpse, as was a wooden chair that "had no mark of fire." Nevertheless, the heat under the woman's burning body must have been intense – the loud crack that had awoken Mrs Roper was the sound of the stone hearth splitting clean across its center. (This feature of the heat being directed downward rather than, as one might logically expect, upward, is common to other SHC reports – e.g. Mary Reeser (1951), Mrs Peacock (1780), Hannah Bradshaw (1770).)

From the position of the body by the fireplace, the cause of the blaze might have seemed obvious but close inspection convinced Dr Newell that the fire had been unlit when Jane Lappiter died. The widow's tobacco pipe (like that of Grace Pett in 1744), was also suspected to be the ignition source but Newell found it empty and neatly "standing upright upon the iron of the grate."

After careful examination of the body and the scene of the accident, Dr Newell concluded that it was "probable that the combustion originated in the body itself, the causes of which, we are at present unacquainted with." The article went on to note: "the most striking and important peculiarity in this case was the manner in which the combustion spread, or extended itself. The burned parts were separated from the skin and the flesh that were uninjured, by an accurately defined line, on one side of which, utter destruction had taken place, while immediately adjoining, there was not the smallest injury done, the skin being sound and natural." He went on to note that the type of burning seen in Jane Lappiter's body reminded him of the way coal smoulders in a hot, but flameless, fire. He believed SHC heat "spreads itself the same way, by a perfectly defined line, reducing in its progress, to ashes, the portions it comes into contact with."

Of course, this was pure conjecture. Nevertheless, it was about the most perceptive guess so far. It certainly explains why so many victims of apparent SHC are reduced to ash – which as we saw in the first chapter takes several hours at over 2,000°C for a crematorium furnace to achieve – yet the resulting heat still does not burn items nearby. Smouldering heat, like that seen in red-hot coals, or the tips of cigarettes, has a very localized damage radius. This is why cigarette stubs do not ignite people's noses and why Hawaiian fire-walkers will suffer no damage to their bare feet provided they do not pause as they cross the fire pit.

Dr Newell concluded that "the peculiar condition under which Spontaneous Combustion takes place, we have no means of knowing; but that some important change must be induced, there can be no doubt; for if the body, in its ordinary state, was capable of taking it on, it would be a frequent occurrence, instead of its being so extremely rare."

Unfortunately, Spontaneous Human Combustion was not so rare that year. In *The Transylvania Journal* (1830), Dr Charles Short gives an account of the apparent SHC of an unnamed woman in Lexington, Kentucky, on November 15, 1829. The victim was in her late 60s, he wrote, and was a drinker. She was found lying in her fireplace and was so severely incinerated that she was at first "mistaken for a piece of wood" – the entire corpse had been reduced to no more than 30 pounds. The fact that she was found lying in a fireplace might have suggested that she had fallen into a blazing fire, but Dr Short pointed out that a potato found in the hearth was still raw.

On Christmas Day that same year, there was another Spontaneous Combustion in Paris. Maria Jeanne Antoinette Bally, a 51-year-old alcoholic, was reduced to a pile of ash, charred bone and a pair of stockinged legs. The remains were found sitting in a chair in a seven-by-ten-foot room that showed little or no fire damage.

Six years later, there was another double fire death. On September 6, 1836, Bernard Lariviere (aged 73), and his wife (aged 65), burned to death in their home at Commune de Surville. A Dr Joly inspected the scene and presented his findings in the *Journal des Connaissances Medico-Chirurgicales* (1836). He himself was quite certain that the couple died of Spontaneous Combustion. Entering the death chamber, he found the pair lying one across the other forming a blackened X on the floor. Of two human beings, he recovered only two pairs of stockinged legs (each burned off an inch above the knee), and a mass of ashes and calcined bones which he calculated to weigh no more than four pounds. Conducting an autopsy by sifting the remains with his hands, the doctor found the victims' lungs and livers shrunk down to a fraction of their normal size. Their brains, he added, were "about the size of hen's eggs." He did not mention whether the skulls were also shrunken – a pity because it might have shed light on Mary Reeser's "orange-sized" skull.

Examining the rest of the room, Dr Joly noted a "strong empyreumic smell" in the air. A chair and its straw cushion were only partially burned, although they were only a few inches from the pile of ashes. Even more bizarre, just above the incinerated couple, was a broom "made of rush, which was scarcely singed on one side, and some matches, the sulphurous end of which projected beyond a clog that contained them." There could hardly be clearer proof that Spontaneous Combustion does not produce ordinary heat. Collecting neighbors' statements, Joly estimated that the Larivieres could have been dead for no more than 14 hours.

Within a month of the death of the Larivieres, "a very fat woman, aged 74 [and] addicted to drinking brandy," burned to death in her home in Auney, in France. The mayor of the town had her door broken down after neighbors said that they were worried because they had not seen her for some time. Her body was found lying by the hearth, reduced to "a heap of something burnt to cinders, at the end of which was a head, a neck, the upper part of a body, and one arm. At the other end were some of the lower parts, and one leg still retaining a very clean shoe and stocking." A blue flame continued to play along a trail of grease or (probably) melted human fat and refused to be snuffed out. The *Medico-Chirurgical Review* hazarded a guess that the drunken woman had been kneeling to blow on the coals when the alcohol vapor on her breath caught fire and ignited her insides – a singularly unlikely scenario.

SHC deaths continued to be reported as the century progressed. Larry Arnold's *Ablaze!* (1995) – the most thorough study of the history of SHC presently available – lists ten SHC deaths over the 11 years between 1836 and 1847. Of these, three victims were French, three German and one each in Belgium, England, New York and Algiers. The regularity and territoriality of SHC reports is, once again, striking. All of these cases displayed typical SHC symptoms, but the Algerian death stands out for two reasons – it is the first African Spontaneous Combustion on record and it was witnessed by several people.

In October 1839, a middle-aged Arab called Abdallah Ben-Ali collapsed in flame in front of onlookers in Algiers. Dr Bubbe-Lievin reported in the *Journal des Connaissances Medicales* that by the time the flames were extinguished, three-quarters of Ben-Ali's body had been destroyed. Witnesses claimed that the flames were of an unusual bluish color. The tint of a flame can indicate to a chemist what the fire is feeding on and blue flames are often mentioned in SHC reports. It is also true that most types of alcohol burn with a blue flame but, as we will see in the next chapter, there are other possibilities that deserve to be considered.

Until the mid-nineteenth century, the medical and legal professions were (on the whole) willing to credit reports of Spontaneous Combustion. Then, in 1847, a single death effectively ended the positive consensus and created the skeptical attitude in these professions that is widespread today.

On June 13, 1847, the German Count von Gorlitz returned from an afternoon party to find his wife had locked herself in her bedroom. Since he was accustomed to his spouse spending periods of solitude in her chamber, he did not disturb her. At 11.00 p.m. he tried knocking and became alarmed when she made no answer. He called his servants and ordered them to break down the door. The Countess was lying on the floor obviously dead. Her lower extremities were unharmed but her torso, arms and head were severely burned. Several nearby pieces of furniture were also fire damaged and flames still played across her writing desk.

The Countess's physician, Dr J.A. Graff, was called and he examined her body. The torso was deeply lacerated by the action of the flames and the flesh on the joints of her arms had fallen away completely. Her blackened head was thrown back with the mouth gaping and the tongue distended. As severe as the fire had evidently been, however, the burning had not reduced her flesh to ash nor were her bones heat-damaged. Nevertheless, Dr Graff recorded the cause of death as "Spontaneous Human Combustion."

That left many people outraged and unconvinced – they believed the Countess had been murdered. An exhumation was carried out and the corpse once again examined, This time, a long crack in her skull was exposed and doctors decided this was nothing to do with the fire. Suspicion immediately fell on her manservant, Stauff, who was known to have been a thief before entering her service. The man was placed on trial, charged with killing his mistress and then trying to cover up the crime by burning her body.

In fact, the court (thanks to the forensic evidence offered by the famous chemist, Baron von Liebig) acquitted Stauff. And at that point, to everyone's astonishment, he made a full confession, claiming that he had heaped various combustible materials on the body and set it alight. Since it is hard to explain why a man who has just been acquitted should deliberately place himself in double jeopardy, it seems likely that the confession was forced out of him by either physical or mental pressure. At all events, he was sentenced to life-imprisonment.

The trial was followed intently in the European and American press and the evidence of Liebig caused intense controversy in the scientific community. Von Liebig was one of the founders of organic chemistry, inventor of the Liebig condenser familiar to every schoolboy, and an expert on the study of carbon compounds. When it came to the effects of fire and carbonization, his reputation was second to none. So when he told the court that his own experiments (essentially the same as Julia de Fontanelle conducted in 1828), showed that Stauff could not have ignited a human body, his opinion carried tremendous weight. Now, although Liebig appeared for the defense in the murder trial, he was not a supporter of Dr Graff's diagnosis of Spontaneous Combustion. In attempting and failing to reduce meat to ash – with or without soaking in alcohol – von Liebig had become convinced that SHC was quite impossible. And because of his reputation, Spontaneous Human Combustion suddenly became a subject of ridicule.

This was plainly absurd. All Liebig had proved was what Fontanelle had already established and what common sense tells us – that it is extremely difficult to burn flesh. This has been known throughout human history – otherwise the Trojans would not have placed Hector's body on a funeral pyre but simply applied a match to his toes. But for some reason, Liebig's un-surprising assertion was accepted as a scientific disproof of Spontaneous Combustion and the nineteenth cen-tury congratulated itself for turning its back on super-stition.

Within four years, Liebig's opinion was being used as a stick to beat England's most famous living author, Charles Dickens. In his novel *Bleak House* (serialized between 1852–53), Dickens kills off the villainous miser Krook by Spontaneous Combustion. "The cat stands snarling – not at them; at something on the ground, before the fire. There is very little fire left in the grate, but there is a smouldering suffocating vapor in the room, and a dark greasy coating on the walls and ceiling. The cat remains where they found her, still snarling at the something on the ground, before the fire and between the two chairs. What is it? Hold up the light. Here is a small burnt patch of flooring; here is the tinder from a little bundle of burnt paper, and here is – is it the cinder of a small charred and broken log of wood sprinkled with white ashes, or is it coal? O Horror, he is here!"

This grim scene affronted the senses of many of Dickens's Victorian readers, but the scientific commu-nity was indignant for another reason. The noted rationalist George Henry Lewes lost no time in writing to *The Leader* magazine to say that he "objected to the episode of Krook's death by Spontaneous Combustion as overstepping the limits of fiction and giving curren-cy to a vulgar error." Dickens replied in the introduc-tion to the first edition of *Bleak House*, explaining: "I have no need to observe that I do not wilfully or

*Depiction of Krook's death in Charles Dickens's classic novel,
Bleak House.*

negligently mislead my readers and that before I wrote that description I took pains to investigate the subject." He went on to mention that he had studied 30 cases, including that of Countess Bandi (1731), on whose death chamber he had based his description of Krook's bedroom.

Oddly enough, Dickens chose not to mention that he had been indirectly involved in a case of Spontaneous Combustion. As a junior reporter, he had written about a coroner's investigation of a likely SHC death. Although the court had arrived at a verdict of death by misadventure, the evidence Dickens had heard convinced him of the reality of Spontaneous Human Combustion. Like most rationalists Lewes paid no attention to the evidence, feeling that reason alone was sufficient to disprove anything so absurd. His attacks led Dickens's friend Forster to write to the *Fortnightly Review* to accuse Lewes of being "odious by intolerable assumptions of an indulgent superiority."

But even Dickens's reputation, and his appeal to actual cases, failed to convince the medical profession. Lewes revealed that he was basing his opinion on Liebig's conclusions, when he declared: "I believe you will not find one eminent organic chemist who credits Spontaneous Combustion." And, unfortunately, he was correct. From that day to this, Spontaneous Combustion has been dismissed as a scientific impossibility.

4

SHC in the Modern World

As the nineteenth century progressed, scientists became increasingly irritated by reports of Spontaneous Human Combustion. The laws on the dissection of corpses had been relaxed since the days of those famous body-snatchers Burke and Hare and this, combined with the availability of modern furnaces, made it clear just how difficult it was to consume a human body. During the 1870s – when the cremation of the dead became fashionable in Europe and the USA – a wealth of new data became available from crematoria and the notion of Spontaneous Human Combustion suddenly seemed an absurdity. By the beginning of the twentieth century, it was regarded as a myth.

However, the general public never had any doubt that Spontaneous Combustion was possible and that the basic cause was "the demon drink." Religious evangelists and temperance crusaders had no reason to contradict this popular belief – it was a useful way of scaring drunks into sobriety – and their missionary zeal had the effect of irritating scientific agnostics still further.

In their book *Spontaneous Human Combustion* (1992), Jenny Randles and Peter Hough list 111 cases of apparent Spontaneous Combustion – of these, 26 came from the 237-year period before 1850 and the remaining 85 were recorded after that date. This might, of course, indicate that SHC was becoming more common but is more likely to be a matter of better documentation, particularly in newspapers. Nowadays, it can be reckoned that the latest cases will be reported in journals devoted to "anomalies," such as the *Fortean Times*. Since it would be impossible to discuss 80 or so cases in this chapter, we shall focus only on the more remarkable ones.

The case of the Parisian house painter referred to in the *Gazette des Triunaux* as "Xavier C" certainly qualifies. In February 1850, in a state of alcoholic exuberance, Xavier bet his drinking companions (in a tavern near the Etoile) that he could eat a lighted candle stub whole. It was to prove a fatal mistake. "Scarcely had he placed it in his mouth, when he uttered a slight cry, and a bluish flame was seen to flicker about his lips, and on an attempt being made to offer him assistance the bystanders were horrified to realize that he was burning internally. At the end of half an hour his head and upper chest were reduced to charcoal. The fire did not cease until the bones, skin and muscles were all consumed, and nothing remained but a small heap of ashes."

We are reminded of other cases. The bluish flame is reminiscent of the fire that consumed the Abdallah Ben-Ali in 1839 and the flame that sprouted from Professor Hamilton's leg. A blue colored flame was also reported in the case of the carbonized woman of Aunay, who was also described as having caused the internal fire by breathing on a naked flame after imbibing a large quantity of alcohol.

In a case cited by Thomas Bartholini in 1654, it was a corpse that burst into flame. While a doctor was performing a post-mortem, a fire suddenly broke out in the woman's opened belly. Bartholini speculated that this may have been caused by alcohol in the woman's stomach, but modern researchers have suggested that the combustible gases in her decomposing intestines might have ignited on exposure to the air. (We will look at the theory of "phosphinic farts" in the next chapter.)

Another case of post-mortem SHC was recorded in 1866. A 30-year-old Englishman had died of typhoid and had been buried in the vault beneath his local church. 13 months later, a foul stench was detected rising from the floor. When the flags were taken up, it was found that his coffin had burst. Sawdust was poured into it and it was replaced in the crypt. The next morning, the floor above the coffin was found to be burning with a bluish flame and the place smelt worse than ever. It was concluded either that the sawdust had started a chemical reaction that started a fire or that a workman had dropped a lighted match or cigarette while filling the coffin with sawdust.

Then there was the curious case of the 66-year-old drunkard who shot himself in the chest with an old fashioned muzzle-loading pistol in October 1885. A doctor named Middlekamp reported the suicide in the *St Louis Medical and Surgical Journal*, and noted that the shot appeared to have started a fire inside the man's lungs (which were probably full of alcohol vapor). The corpse went on burning until only the legs, head and arms remained. But clearly this was not an ordinary fire. It burned so fiercely that a metal buckle as well as the iron ramrod (which the dead man had failed to remove from the barrel before firing), were found partially melted in the ashes.

The potential risk of being near an SHC death, even if you are in another room, was highlighted by the case of Patrick and Matilda Rooney. This prosperous farming couple, both 72, lived in Ottawa – a little rural town 65 miles from Chicago. On Christmas Eve 1885, the Rooneys were drinking whisky in the kitchen with their live-in farmhand, John Larson. After a couple of drinks, Larson decided to go to bed and left Mr and Mrs Rooney to toast the season alone. In the middle of the night, he woke up choking and gasping for breath but put it down to a bad cold and soon managed to get back to sleep. The next morning, Larson came down from his room (which was just above the kitchen) and found Patrick Rooney lying dead in his ground floor bedroom. A hasty search showed no sign of Mrs Rooney, so Larson concluded that she must have killed her husband and fled. It was only when he returned with the police that Matilda Rooney was found. She was in a hole in the kitchen floor.

The *Ottawa Daily Republican Times* reported that "there was a hole burned through the floor four feet in length and three in breadth through which the incinerated remains had fallen." The pine floorboards were an inch thick. Gingerly probing the contents of the hole, searchers "found a calcined skull, part of a vertebral column and a handful of white ashes." The *Ottawa Free Trader Journal* added that the flesh had been entirely consumed except that part which covered the bones of one foot. "The foot was found just at the edge of the aperture in the floor, through which the body had disappeared. The limb had burned slowly to the ankle – flesh and bone – and when the body dropped the charred bone snapped, and the foot with the shoe intact, righted itself and stood up as if its owner had been burned at the stake." Nothing in the room was burned except Mrs Rooney's body, the hole in the floor and the tablecloth fringe. Here, as in the case of Countess Bandi, a woman had burned to ash either standing or squatting with her feet flat on the floor.

Looking around the kitchen, they saw that "the walls were blackened as if with lampblack, as was the floor and the woodwork." This indicated a lot of smoke, but surely Larson could not have failed to notice the distinct smell of burning flesh, even if he did have a cold? In fact, Larson said he smelt nothing so it is likely Mrs Rooney's death blaze was as odorless as that of Mary Reeser (described in chapter 1).

And what of Patrick Rooney? The autopsy revealed that he had died of suffocation. When Larson's bedroom was inspected it was found that his pillow was smoke blackened. It seems clear that he would also have died of suffocation if he had not been upstairs. Indeed Larson, who was no longer young, died just two weeks later. The coroner ruled that his death was caused by "the poison inhaled that night."

Another extraordinary case was described by Dr J. Mackenzie Booth when he addressed the Aberdeen Branch of the British Medical Association on March 21, 1888. The subject of his talk was a death he had been called on to certify on the morning of the previous February 19. The deceased was a 65-year-old ex-soldier of "notoriously intemperate habits," whom Booth referred to only as "A.M.". At around 9.00 p.m., two children had seen him climb the ladder (in an obviously drunken condition) into the stable hayloft. Shortly afterwards, they said they saw a glow coming from the skylight but this was soon extinguished. The following morning, between 8 and 9.00 a.m., the stable owner saw smoke drifting from a hole in the roof. He hurried to extinguish the fire but nothing was burning. He did, nevertheless, find A.M.'s blackened corpse, sitting on the joists of the stable ceiling. The police were called and they in turn called in Dr Booth. As far as Booth could tell, the old soldier had burned his way clean through the hayloft floor and landed on the ceiling joist of the room below, with his back remaining propped against the wall. Only the burned floorboards and an area of the roof directly above the dead man's head were affected by the fire. Most extraordinary of all was the fact that the dry straw in the hayloft had not ignited.

As to the burnt soldier, Dr Booth told his colleagues that "the body was itself almost a cinder, yet retaining the form of the face and figure so well, that those who had known him in life could readily recognize him.

"Both hands and the right foot had been burnt off and had fallen through the floor among the ashes into the stable below, and the charred and calcined ends of the right radius and ulna, the left humerus, and the right tibia and fibula were exposed to view. The hair and scalp were burnt off the forehead, exposing the bare and calcined skull. The tissues of the face were

The 'old soldier' in the hayloft in Aberdeen, Scotland, in 1888

represented by a greasy cinder retaining the cast of the features and the incinerated moustache still gave the wonted military expression to the old soldier. The soft tissues were almost entirely consumed, more especially on the posterior surface of the body." A.M. had not suffered in dying, Dr Booth assured his audience: "from the comfortably recumbent attitude of the body it was evident that there had been no death struggle." The old drunk "obfuscated by whisky within and smoke without, had expired without suffering, the body burning away quietly all the time."

Unfortunately, when the policemen tried to move the corpse from its undignified perch the front of the head collapsed, destroying the perfect death mask. Before they tried again, a Mr W. Reid took a picture of the body using a camera obscura and one of the newly invented light sensitive calotype plates. This is the first known photograph of a SHC victim. Booth added that A.M. was so desiccated that "the whole body collapsed when they tried to move it *en masse.*" Thus the only surviving evidence was Reid's photograph, the hole in the hayloft floor and a heap of greasy ashes.

Another unusual case of Spontaneous Human Combustion was reported by Dr B.H. Hartwell in the *Boston Medical and Surgical Journal* for 1890. Hartwell had virtually stumbled on the body of a 49-year-old Massachusetts woman in a wood. On the afternoon of May 12 he was out on a professional call when, as the road passed through a patch of woodland, he found himself looking down at the dead woman lying on the ground. "The body was face downward; the face, arms, upper part of the chest, and left knee only touching the ground; the rest of the body was raised and held from the ground by the rigidity of the muscles of the parts. It was burning at the shoulder, both sides of the abdomen, and both legs. The flames reached from 12 to 15 inches above the level of the body. The clothing was nearly all consumed. As I reached the spot the bones of the right leg broke with an audible snap, allowing the foot to hang by the tendons and muscles of one side, those of the other side having burned completely off. Sending my driver for water and assistance, I could only watch the curious and abhorrent spectacle, till a common spading fork was found with which the fire was put out by throwing earth upon it."

When the corpse had cooled, Dr Hartwell was able to make an examination. The flesh was burned from the right shoulder, he noted, and an area of flesh was also burned from the abdomen, allowing the intestines to protrude. The legs were all but stripped of flesh and the leg bones were partially calcined. Yet, despite the virulence of the fire, parts of her cotton vest, woollen skirt and thick woollen undergarments had survived. It seemed that the woman had set fire to a pile of roots and woodland litter shortly before she died, but she was lying over 30 feet away from the bonfire. The possibility that the flames had somehow travelled along the ground to her dress was also highly unlikely, since it had rained shortly before the doctor came upon her. Hartwell believed that this woman's death and subsequent burning indicated "preternatural combustion" (from an outside source). In his opinion, it proved "that under certain conditions – conditions that exist in the body itself – the human body will burn, and this has given rise to the belief in the spontaneous origin of the fire." He added that the woman was known to be a non-drinker.

So far, most of the cases we have considered have involved the elderly – Spontaneous Combustion involving children is a rarity. Yet a case cited by Jenny Randles and Peter Hough is surely one of the most bizarre ever recorded. It took place in Sowerby Bridge, West Yorkshire, England, in 1899. The victims, Alice and Amy Kirby, were five and four-years-old respectively. They lived with their parents, Sara and John, but not together. Mr and Mrs Kirby had separated and lived in different houses, each with one child. John Kirby took the older girl to live with him and her grandmother at 45 Wakefield Road, while Amy stayed with her mother at the family's original house on Hargreaves Terrace. Nevertheless, the two houses were only a mile apart across the Calder Valley.

At about 11.00 a.m. on January 5, Sara Kirby went with a bucket to the well 20 yards from her front door. It was raining, so she ran and it took her no more than two minutes to return. As she entered the house, Amy was screaming, and the mother found her bathed in flames. At the subsequent inquest, Mrs Kirby told the court that "if [Amy] had had paraffin oil thrown over her she would not have burned faster." The flames reached three feet above the little girl's head.

When the child was extinguished and an ambulance sent for, the hysterical Sara Kirby set out on foot to take the news to her husband and other daughter. She had not reached Wakefield Road, however, before a messenger met her coming the other way. At exactly the same moment that Amy caught fire – 11.00 a.m. – so had five-year-old Alice. And both girls died before the day was out. The coroner heard that Amy had an extreme fear of fire and was unlikely to have been playing with matches, while Alice was lying in bed when her body burst into flame. No source of ignition could be found at either scene.

Now we can see that this case is perhaps the most baffling we have considered so far. Both girls burst into flame at the same time. If they had been identical twins, this might have been slightly more credible for research since the late 1970s has established beyond all doubt that some strange connection exists between identical twins. Twins named Barbara Herbert and Daphne Goodfield, who met for the first time as adults, were wearing identical costumes when they met at King's Cross station. But this only proved to be the first of a series of unbelievable coincidences. Both were local government workers, both had met their husbands at a dance at the age of 16 and married early, both had suffered a miscarriage with their first baby then both had two boys, both had fallen downstairs at the age of 15, both read the same women's magazines and had the same favorite authors. And since a social worker named John Stroud publicized the case, dozens more have appeared. An American pair of male twins had both married a girl called Linda, then divorced and married a girl called Betty, both had sons called John Allan and both spent their holidays at the same resort in Florida and used the same beach – although they had never met. An American psychologist named Tim Bouchard who obtained a grant to study identical twins soon discovered that such coincidences are not the exception but the rule. They cannot be explained by their genetic identity, for all logic agrees that this cannot possibly extend to their

---

Malignant hyperthermia is the medical term for the metabolic superheating of the human body. A person's "normal" temperature is 98.6°F (37°C). A feverish 109°F (42.7°C) is known to generally be fatal if sustained for any amount of time. Nevertheless, people have been known to survive much higher body temperatures.

The *Guinness Book of World Records* notes that a Mr Willie Jones survived a fever of 115.7°F (46.5°C) in Atlanta in 1980, but this seems positively cool compared to other recorded cases. The *Clinical Society of London* noted, in 1875, that a woman survived four days at 122°F (50°C). And in 1888 a woman in Guy's Hospital, London, reached 130°F (54.4°C) – hospital thermometers did not go this high, so doctors had to use a horse thermometer.

The most shocking cases, however, were recorded at the 1895 meeting of the Association of American Physicians. A Dr Jacobi first reported on the case of a New York fireman who, following a fall, reached a comatose temperature of 148°F (64.4°C). Murmurs of disbelief were stilled when a Dr Welch of Baltimore arose to report on a closely monitored and well-documented case of a fever reaching 171°F (77.2°C).

At 212°F (100°C) water starts to steam. Is it possible that rampant fevers are the cause of Spontaneous Human Combustion?

"fate" or destiny. Yet apparently it does. There seems to be some mysterious "connection" which, for want of a better word, we have to label "psychic."

The case of the two Kirby girls seems to demand a similar explanation – that there was some "connection" that caused them to burst into flame at the same time. That, in turn, makes us wonder if Spontaneous Combustion is not simply some physical mystery but whether the mind plays an equally important role in it.

This is something that must be discussed in the next chapter. But at this point, I can at least offer a suggestion. "Poltergeists" (or "noisy ghosts") are among the best authenticated of psychic phenomena – thousands of cases have been observed and recorded. They make banging noises, cause objects to fly across the room, pools of water to form out of nowhere and occasionally they throw people out of bed. In the twentieth century, the most fashionable theory has been that they are due to the unconscious psychic powers of disturbed children and teenagers. The power to move objects by the mind alone is known at "psychokinesis" (or PK), and psychical researchers are mostly inclined to believe that this is what happens in poltergeist phenomena. The unconscious powers of the teenager somehow make things "happen." The only objection to this theory is that when PK takes place in the laboratory, it involves moving such tiny things as compass needles or fragments of paper. But poltergeists have even been known to lift a Land Rover!

Now an increasing number of "parapsychologists" are beginning to admit – reluctantly – that poltergeists may be "spirits" who somehow use the emotional energy of disturbed human beings. In fact, this was the view that was held during the nineteenth century. A French scholar named Hyppolyte Rivail heard of two young girls who practised "automatic writing" and had no doubt that their hands were controlled by spirits. Rivail had "sittings" with these girls and asked the "spirits" various questions, to which the answers were written down. And the intelligence and consistency of these answers soon convinced Rivail that he was genuinely in touch with spirits.

Now there had been some extraordinary poltergeist activity in a house in the Rue Noyers, which had finally driven the tenants to leave. Denizard asked the "spirits" about this "haunting" and the "control" (the spirit who acts as master of ceremonies) summoned the poltergeist, who was at first rude and aggressive. It claimed to be the spirit of a drunken rag and bone man, who was taking his revenge for the way he was treated while alive. Rivail asked where the poltergeist had obtained its energy and it explained that it had made use of a servant girl. Rivail asked if she was aware she was being "used" and the spirit replied that, on the contrary, she was more terrified than anyone. Asked how the spirit made use of the girl to throw objects across the room, it replied, "I helped myself through the electric nature of the girl, joined to my own. Thus we were able to transport objects between us."

Rivail wrote it all down in a work called *The Spirits' Book*, using the pseudonym Allan Kardec. It is still one of the most fascinating books ever written on the subject of the paranormal. What is so interesting here is this suggestion that the spirit used the girl's "electric nature." There have been (as we shall see later) dozens of cases of "human magnets" who cause metal to stick to them, and human electric eels who can give people a stunning shock and even knock them unconscious.

Is it possible that the basic force that drives all animals is some kind of electrical force? It seems an absurd idea – there is nothing obviously "electrical" about most of us. Yet a child would say the same about an electric light or television set or vacuum cleaner. Yet if a wire comes loose and the child touches it, he suddenly realizes that they are driven by an invisible electrical force. Is it possible that the same is true of human beings and that Spontaneous Combustion is some kind of short circuit that starts a fire? It is also worth bearing in mind that one of the tricks that poltergeists love to play is starting fires. Presumably they do this by using the same "electrical force" that the Rue Noyers poltergeist mentioned.

Six years after the tragedy that struck the Kirby family, unknown forces of the poltergeist variety besieged Binbrook Farm in Lincolnshire. Harry Price, a founder of modern parapsychological research, notes in his book *Poltergeist* that throughout December and January 1904–5, Binbrook Farm suffered flying objects, a strange "pressure" in and around the house and spontaneous, inexplicable fires.

Most poltergeist phenomena, for all their apparent violence, are relatively harmless. Heavy objects hurtle across the room and smash against the wall, missing someone's head by an eighth of an inch. In this case, however, the strange force was positively murderous. The first victims were the farm chickens – these were found in the yard with their throats torn out. Then a blanket in a room burst into flames and might have burned the whole house down if it had not been discovered. Finally, in early January, the farmer (who was called White), walked into his kitchen and saw the serving maid engaged in sweeping the floor while the back of her dress was on fire. White told the *Louth and North Lincolnshire News* that she was quite unaware of her danger. "She looked around as I shouted, and, seeing the flames, rushed through the door. She tripped, and I smothered the fire out with wet sacks. But she was terribly burned." The reader may recall the similar case in chapter 2, when an English gentleman came upon the kitchen maid scrubbing the floor, unaware that her back was alight. The girl died while fortunately, farmer White's servant survived.

In his book *Fire From Heaven*, Michael Harrison notes an equally curious incident in the London borough of Sydenham during the summer of 1922. 68-year-old Euphemia Johnson had just returned home from a shopping trip and had made a cup of tea. The widow carried the cup to a table with a view out the window but never drank it. She was found on the floor, reduced to a pile of ash and calcined bone lying in her *undamaged* clothing. Beside the body was a fallen chair on which the varnish was only slightly heat blistered. The rubberized tablecloth above her was quite unharmed – although it was highly inflammable.

Harrison cites a parallel case which took place on the island of Antigua in the West Indies, in 1929. Here the clothes of a young woman called Lily White kept bursting into flame, leaving her partially clothed or naked but otherwise quite unharmed. These Spontaneous Combustions took place in the street as well as indoors and sometimes would also affect her bedclothes. Numerous witnesses testified that the fires appeared to be totally spontaneous.

A similar case took place in Bladenboro, North Carolina, in January 1932. A Mrs Williamson's cotton dress suddenly burst into flame although there was no heat source in her vicinity. Her husband Charles and their daughter tore the burning dress from her body but, to their relief and amazement, neither she nor they suffered a single burn. In this case, there is a strong possibility that the Williamsons were the subject of a poltergeist attack, for the next day Mr Williamson's trousers burst into flame in a closed wardrobe. A bed also caught fire and a fire started in an unoccupied room. Other articles burst into flame and burned without touching nearby objects. The flames could not be smothered but suddenly vanished of their own accord. The fire brigade and the police investigated without result. After four days, the Williamsons moved out and the fires stopped. Michael Harrison does not mention the age of the daughter, but it sounds as if she might well have been the "focus" of poltergeist activity.

Many more deaths by Spontaneous Combustion are recorded in the 1930s and 1940s than in any previous period, both in England and the USA. In July 1938, Mrs Mary Carpenter burst into flames while travelling in a cabin cruiser on the Norfolk Broads and was reduced to a charred corpse in moments.

On August 27, 1938, 22-year-old Phyllis Newcombe was engulfed in flames while dancing with her boyfriend in Chelmsford, Essex, and died soon after. It was thought that a cigarette might have caused the fire but tests showed that the material of her dress was too flameresistant to ignite in this way.

On January 4, 1939, 11-month-old Peter Seaton was burned to death in his nursery. Between his first scream and the time it took to run upstairs, Peter's room was completely engulfed in flames. Opening his door was like opening "the door of a furnace," said an eyewitness. The baby's body was completely destroyed. The London Fire Brigade could find no cause for the inferno.

Allen M. Small was found dead in his home on Deer Island, Maine, on January 13, 1943. His body and the carpet directly beneath him were badly burned but nothing else showed signs of a fire. No ignition source could be found.

Sussex woman, Madge Knight, was lying asleep in bed on the night of December 6, 1943, when her back suddenly burst into flame. She was rushed to Chichester hospital but was too badly burned to survive. Her bedclothes, however, were found to be totally unscorched.

Six years later, Mrs Ellen K. Coutres, 53, was found dead in her home in Manchester, New Hampshire. She had apparently burned like a human torch but the wooden house was quite unaffected. The authorities could find no reason for the blaze.

On May 3, 1951, the first known Spontaneous Human Combustion in a car took place in Indiana. A passing motorist spotted the car of Carl C. Blocker sitting parked by the side of State Road 15 between

Wabash and Syracuse. In a nearby ditch was Blocker, burning furiously. The motorist extinguished the fire and Blocker was rushed to hospital, but he was too badly burned and died without regaining consciousness. Police investigation of the car indicated that Blocker had started to burn while sitting behind the wheel. Although most of the car was undamaged, the driver's seat was badly burnt and "the heat had been so bad it had started to melt the metal instrument panel." Investigation of the 44-year-old family man ruled out either suicide or murder. Blocker ran several successful clothes shops and detectives briefly considered the possibility that flammable cleaning chemicals might be to blame. Forensic examination and Mrs Blocker's assurance that her husband never carried such materials in his car, however, left the investigation with no further leads.

Blocker's death occurred two months before Mary Reeser was burned in her room in Florida. In that case, the police suspected lightning, but finally had to rule it out. The same is true of the Blocker case. Because of the rubber tyres, a car is a kind of Faraday Cage – that is, a structure that completely protects the occupants from lightning or other energy transmissions. In over 100 years of automobile use around the world, there has not been a single report of someone being struck by lightning in a car. In a thunderstorm, the safest place is inside a car.

Over the next three years, three more American men died in mysterious fires in their vehicles. On June 30, 1952, a man was found burned beyond recognition in an unharmed car at Wallace, Idaho.

On March 1, 1953, Waymon P. Wood was found "crisped black" in a closed car off Bypass Route 291 in Greenville, South Carolina. Researcher Frank Edwards reported that Wood's corpse was totally gutted by "a fire of undetermined origin," and that "the plastic fittings had melted and the windshield had bubbled and sagged into the car. Yet the fire itself had been confined to the front seat."

Larry Arnold reports another strange car death from 1953. In early April, Maryland police found the car of Bernard J. Hess overturned at the bottom of a 20-foot embankment in Arundel County, 15 miles southeast of Baltimore. Initially, the cause of death appeared to be an obvious wound to Hess's head. Yet when the county coroner undressed the man for the autopsy, he found him to be covered with fresh, first and second degree burns over about two-thirds of his body. The police had missed this fact because Hess's clothes were quite unburned, as was his car.

The age and weight of SHC victims have often been thought to be an important factor. As we have seen, the majority of cases have involved elderly, overweight women, most of whom drank too much. Some researchers have suggested that the sedentary lifestyle of such women might be an indirect cause of the Spontaneous Combustion. Could it be that they build up some chemicals in the skin or gas in their intestines? Or could it be, as Jenny Randles and Peter Hough suggest, that a sedentary lifestyle causes a build up of static electricity?

The case of a Honolulu man called Young Sik may be cited in support of this view. Aged 78 and totally

*The remains of Dr John Irving Bentley, December 1966
(copyright 1976/1993 by Larry E. Arnold)*

wheelchair bound, he was found enveloped in blue flame in December 1956. It took firemen only 15 minutes to arrive but by that time, Mr Sik and his wheelchair had been reduced to a pile of ashes. Nothing else in his room was damaged by the intense blaze.

On December 13, 1959, another American died in his car but this time the cause of death was clear – suicide by the inhalation of exhaust gas. Billy Peterson died in his garage with a hose running from the exhaust pipe into the car. Smoke coming from under the garage door alerted a passing motorist to the tragedy. Billy's corpse, however, was severely burned around the nose, mouth, ears, arms and genitals. The heat of the blaze had been so intense that a plastic statue on the dashboard had melted but Billy's clothes were not even scorched. It was suggested that the gas that had killed him was somehow responsible for the fire damage, until someone pointed out that carbon monoxide is a fire-retardant.

Just after 9.00 a.m. on December 5, 1966, gas man Don Gosnell entered 403 North Main Street in Coudersport, Pennsylvania – the home of 92-year-old Dr John Irving Bentley. Gosnell did not bother to knock, since he had previously been told to simply let himself in when it was time to read the meter. He did, however, call out to the doctor as he passed the door to the old man's apartment but got no reply. As he walked down the corridor towards the cellar door, Gosnell noticed a light-blue smoke in the air with "a strange, sickening sweet odor that I wasn't familiar with." The closest he could liken it to was the smell of "a new heating system – an oil-film burning, somewhat sweet." (The reader may recollect that this sounds like the description given by Pansy Carpenter of the sweetish, "over-heating electric motor" smell caused by the Spontaneous Combustion of Mary Reeser.)

In the cellar, Gosnell found a five-inch high pile of ashes beneath a burned two-by-four-foot hole in the boards of the ceiling. There was no further sign of fire but the three-inch-thick oak boards were still glowing cherry-red around the edges of the hole. The room above was Dr Bentley's bathroom. There Gosnell found the doctor's walking frame and a fire-severed lower leg. That, apart from a knee joint and the ashes in the basement, were all that was left of the old man. Nothing beyond the perimeter of the hole – including the flammable, tar-backed floor linoleum – was fire damaged. No ignition source could be found in the bathroom, so the coroner suggested that Dr Bentley had accidentally set his dressing gown on fire with his pipe – an unlikely explanation since Dr Bentley's only pipe was found placed neatly in a stand in his bedroom. The possibility that the doctor had placed it there when he realized he was burning and hurried to the bathroom, was ruled out when his nurse stated that it took the old man five minutes to shuffle between the bedroom and bathroom.

One baffling – and gruesome – case of Spontaneous Combustion was witnessed by several firemen including Fire Brigade Commander John Stacy. At around 5.20 a.m. on September 13, 1967, early morning workers noticed a flickering light coming from an abandoned house in the London borough of Lambeth and raised a fire alarm. Commander Stacy arrived with a fire engine several minutes later and broke into number 49

Auckland Street. They found the body of a 63-year-old tramp, Robert Francis Bailey, lying on the bottom of the stairs half-turned onto his left side. The man had quite clearly died in torment, Stacy recalled in an interview with Larry Arnold, he had bitten deep into a solid mahogany stair-post. "His knees were drawn up as though he was trying to bend the pain from his stomach." The cause of the tramp's agony was immediately obvious – a four-inch slit in his stomach, just above the navel, from which flame issued as if from a blowtorch. The now retired fire officer added that the flame was blue in color. "The flame was actually coming from the body itself," Stacy confirmed, "from *inside* the body. He was literally burning from the inside out! And it was definitely under pressure – it was impingeing onto the flooring below the body, so much so that the heat from the flame was charred into the woodwork." It took several fire extinguishers to kill the fire in Robert Bailey's belly.

A fireman is trained to confirm three items when investigating a mystery blaze – the fuel, the supply of oxygen and the ignition source. In Commander Stacy's opinion, the fuel had been the alcohol drunk by Bailey – perhaps methylated spirit which burns with a blue flame. But he admitted being baffled about the ignition source and the oxygen supply, since the fire was inside Bailey's stomach. Although officially the London Fire Brigade discounts the possibility of Spontaneous Human Combustion, Stacy remarked off the record that he believed that this was probably the explanation for Robert Bailey's death. The autopsy led to the conclusion that Bailey had died of "asphyxia due to the inhalation of fire fumes." In other words, he had suffocated on the smoke of his own combustion. The coroner ruled that the cause of the fire was "unknown due to lack of evidence."

Clothing salesman, Jack Angel, is one of the best known SHC survivors of recent years having been featured in many magazine articles and television shows. On the evening of Monday, November 11, 1975, Angel arrived at a motel in Savannah, Georgia, only to be told that his previously booked room had been given to somebody else. Since he was driving a motorhome, he was not particularly bothered and settled down for the night in the bed in the back of the vehicle. When he awoke at about midday, he realized – although he felt no pain – that he was badly burned. His right hand and an area of his chest had suffered third degree burns (the most severe of the three categories). Yet he had no memory of how it had happened. In a state of shock, Angel took a shower and dressed himself. Then he made his way to the motel bar and ordered a scotch. The waitress noticed his blackened right hand and asked what had happened. Angel replied groggily, "Looks like I got burned." Shortly thereafter, he passed out on the way to the toilet.

Rushed to hospital, he remained in a semi-conscious state until his nerves came out of shock and he suffered excruciating pain. The doctors initially refused to answer his questions but were plainly horrified by his injuries. Eventually, one told him that the burns were not the usual kind encountered in emergency departments but seemed to have been somehow generated *inside* the flesh. The damage, whatever the cause, was too extreme to save the hand so surgeons were forced to amputate it at the forearm. The motorhome was checked but no evidence of a fire could be found, even on the bedclothes. The authorities believed that the injuries were due to an accident with either the vehicle's electricity supply or hot water heater, the shock of which had knocked him unconscious and blanked his memory. Since no evidence of such an accident could be found, Jack Angel concluded that he had been a victim of Spontaneous Human Combustion. One of the oddest aspects of this case is the length of time Angel slept – he went to bed on Monday evening and woke up at midday *the following Friday*. Flying saucer enthusiasts have even suggested that Jack Angel was abducted by aliens and that he was the victim of typical "missing time" syndrome. But it is certainly not clear why the aliens should have wanted to inflict burn injuries.

Spontaneous Combustion deaths seem to have been especially plentiful in the 1980s. Jenny Randles and Peter Hough list 21 cases between 1980 and 1990. Most of these have the typical features of Spontaneous Combustion, as in the case of 73-year-old Henry Thomas, discovered in his living room in Ebbw Vale, South Wales on January 6, 1980, completely reduced to ash – apart from his totally undamaged feet. The chair he had been sitting in was destroyed but the rest of the room was undamaged. Even the plastic tiles beneath the carpet were unmelted.

There were also cases of "preternatural combustions," most notably in 1985. At 11.00 a.m. on January

28, 17-year-old Jacqueline Fitzsimon burst into flames walking down the stairs from her cookery class. Although badly burned over her back and shoulders, she started to make a strong recovery, then died suddenly 15 days after the combustion. The coroner's court ruled that she had accidentally ignited her clothes on a gas stove as she queued to leave the class and that the draught on the stairwell caused the smouldering to flare into a blaze. This otherwise convincing explanation failed to take into account the statements of two fellow classmates, who said that a second before the fire started a small blue light had fallen on Jacqueline and moved down her back.

On May 25, 1985, a 19-year-old man was out walking in the streets of Stepney Green, London, when he suddenly burst into flames. He later said that he felt as if he had been doused in burning petrol, but as he rolled on the ground the fire suddenly went out. He was burned but managed to walk to the local casualty department unaided.

The most recent case of apparent SHC (at the time of writing – June 1997) was that of 76-year-old John O'Conner in Gortaleen, County Kerry, in the Republic of Ireland. On March 24, 1997, O'Conner was found burned to death in his living room by the community nurse. His legs, lower torso, hands and arms were severely burnt but there was little smoke damage to the room or furniture. Local priest, Patrick McCarthey, was reported in the *Fortean Times* as saying that it looked as if somebody had poured petrol into his lap.

So, while science in the twentieth century has remained obdurately convinced that Spontaneous

Human Combustion is a myth, more instances have been recorded than in any previous century. Yet we are as far from understanding it as ever. It seems clear that until some university or scientific society can be persuaded to launch a long-term investigation, it is unlikely that we shall come any closer to solving the mystery. However, in the next chapter we shall see how far common sense and ingenuity can suggest an answer.

5

Explanations?

As the policeman looked down at the badly incinerated corpse, his first thought was that the victim had been murdered. Either that or he had committed suicide in a particularly painful way. What puzzled Detective Sergeant Nigel Cruttenden of the Kent police was that a polythene dustpan and brush were only inches away from the body and they had not even started to melt.

The scene mentioned above was a flat above a baker's shop in Folkestone, England, and the victim was 44-year-old Barry Soudain, a handyman who was known to be an alcoholic. There was another odd fact about the death scene. A kettle on a blazing gas-ring was shooting a plume of steam towards the ceiling. Barry Soudain's landlord, Mr Gower, found the boiling kettle when he walked into the kitchen and turned it off. The obvious inference is that Mr Soudain had spontaneously combusted in the half hour since he put the kettle on to boil. The fact that it was still half full of water proved that it had not been on the gas for very long.

Why bother to even mention a case which is virtually identical to so many others in this book? Because the

BBC decided to use it as one of their main examples in a television program entitled "A Case of Spontaneous Human Combustion?" The aim of this program – in the science series "Q.E.D." – was to prove that Spontaneous Human Combustion is nonsense. The theory put forward by the program was that, since a human being contains an enormous amount of fat, he might (under certain circumstances) burn like a candle or smoulder away for hours until he simply disappeared. The program argued that if all the oxygen in a room is used up by the fire, the body could continue smouldering until it had turned into a pile of ash. In that case, the program argued, the rest of the furniture in the room might well remain untouched.

There is only one problem with this theory. For a body to smoulder away until it disappears would take a long time – probably a whole day or night. In the case of Barry Soudain, this is obviously impossible because the kettle had still not boiled dry. But for some reason, this piece of information was not mentioned on the program. This attempt to prove that Spontaneous Human Combustion is an impossibility was fatally flawed.

Jenny Randles and Peter Hough decided to look into the "Q.E.D." theory for their book *Spontaneous Human Combustion*. What they found left them unimpressed. The theory that the body can burn like a candle is the intellectual brainchild of Dr Dougal Drysdale of Edinburgh University. Dr Drysdale later explained to Jenny Randles that, "It's a misconception to think you need [high] temperatures within a living-room to reduce a body in this way. You can produce local high temperatures by means of the wick effect and a combination of smouldering and flaming to *reduce even bones to ash."*

On the program, Dr Drysdale placed an animal bone in a special furnace which would subject it to a temperature of 500°C, with the comment that in about six hours it should be reduced to ash. But even at the end of eight hours, the bone was charred but still recognizable. Dr Drysdale suggested that if it had been left in for another four hours, it would definitely have been reduced to powder. The "Q.E.D." program also tried to demonstrate that an armchair, set alight by a cigarette, could smoulder in an almost airless room until it was reduced to its springs. Their attempt to demonstrate this was also a failure – after six hours of smouldering most of the armchair was still intact.

Dr Drysdale certainly deserves to be given nine out of ten for effort. The problem is that he is contradicted by the basic facts. Most cases of Spontaneous Combustion do *not* take place in closed rooms where lack of oxygen will finally cause smouldering. The majority take place in rooms with plenty of oxygen – for example, those with a chimney. Some even take place in the open air. But apart from that, this book has shown that the majority of cases cannot be dismissed as examples of quite ordinary combustion. Spontaneous Human Combustion seems to be some strange process that starts *inside* the human body and simply consumes human flesh in the way that a fire consumes coal. In other words, either the nature of the fire is quite different from ordinary fire, or some strange process starts in the body that *transforms* flesh into a combustible substance.

Even ordinary firemen seem to recognize that Spontaneous Human Combustion is not a myth. Jenny Randles interviewed the country fire officer for Cleveland, William Cooney, and quotes Cooney as saying, "The fire starts from within the body but the extremities are what survive. I do not believe that you can suffer SHC, if the hand, for example, is the primary source . . . . take the analogy of a bonfire. If we light one of these, then the bits of wood at the edge are what get left – not the pieces in the middle. These are consumed. The fire in SHC always starts from the middle." He added, "In experiments where fat wrapped in cloth has been set alight to demonstrate that the human body could burn like a candle, an external source of heat was applied to get them going. They do not suddenly ignite by themselves do they? That is what makes the reports of SHC so remarkable, because apparently, ignition is 'spontaneous'!"

It seems clear that the BBC were determined to do a program "debunking" Spontaneous Combustion. But the debunking mentality is usually crude and one-sided. One police "scenes of crime" officer, John Haymer, told Jenny Randles, " 'Q.E.D.' was a farce! They came to me and I didn't want to do the program, but they assured me they were doing a serious documentary. So I gave them access to all my records, full details of several cases . . . . when the program was aired, they had completely changed their approach and seemed to be going all out to disprove the phenomenon. I was very annoyed. In fact I tried to phone the producer, but was told she was on holiday abroad. In my opinion, the program did not represent what this phenomenon truly is."

The "phosphinic fart" is perhaps the most disturbing suggested cause of Spontaneous Human Combustion. Phosphor (and phosphine, its hydrogenized gas), bursts into flame when it comes into contact with oxygen. It is a proven fact that the human body can produce phosphoric by-products – in the days before refrigeration, corpses were famous for glowing with phosphorescent "corpse lights." If, under exceptional circumstances, a person's intestines produced and released a puff of pure phosphine, it might easily set their skin on fire.

Cases like that of Mrs Madge Knight, whose back caught fire in bed in 1943, and Jacqueline Fitzsimon, whose back and shoulders caught fire outside her cookery class in 1985, have been suggested to be phosphine-fart-ignited combustion cases. Phosphine gas *inside* a person might also ignite if it comes into contact with enough oxygen, thus starting an internal Spontaneous Human Combustion.

It is significant that the commentary on the "Q.E.D." program assured the viewer that "even in the most bizarre cases there's no need to resort to the supernatural. Science can provide a perfectly rational explanation for all of these deaths." No one, of course, thinks that Spontaneous Combustion is "supernatural." But the comment reveals the peculiar paranoia that besets "skeptics" when they feel that some anomaly challenges their comfortable, rational view of the universe. On the whole, it is probably safe to dismiss the "human candle" view of Spontaneous Combustion since it simply fails to take full account of the facts.

Jenny Randles and Peter Hough seem altogether

closer to a solution when they point out that a haystack can burst into flame because of heat generated inside the damp hay by the chemical processes of decomposition. The heat cannot escape and so builds up. The human body is doing something similar all the time. We eat food and the body transforms this food into energy and waste matter. Alcohol – particularly spirits – is noted for its effect of producing a "warm glow." Is it not possible that (particularly in an obese person), this warm glow could eventually build up like the heat inside a haystack to cause Spontaneous Combustion?

In Issue 52 of the *Fortean Times*, a Dutch chemical engineer called Hugh Stiles pointed out that the water in the human body would not actually be an obstacle to this type of Spontaneous Combustion. He suggests that, with enough internal heat, the soft tissues of the human body – which contain carbon – would oxidize and turn into carbon dioxide. This process would in itself create heat. However, just as it begins to look as if somebody has suggested a believable mechanism for Spontaneous Combustion, a basic objection arises. This heat would cause the water in the human body to evaporate, so rooms in which Spontaneous Combustion has occurred would be thoroughly damp with steam. This has never been known to happen.

Mrs D.G. Viner told Jenny Randles an intriguing story which demonstrates that our insides are not as invulnerable to flame as we might think. She described how she was sitting in bed starting to light a cigarette with a throwaway lighter. Then she heard a rushing noise, rather like the roar of a bunsen burner. "Suddenly I realized my mouth and throat felt very sore and that the sound was coming from me. I quickly clamped a hand over my mouth only to find this channelled the sensation through my nose. I pinched my nostrils together and this stopped the rushing feeling and the bunsen burner sound. Gradually I lessened the pressure on my nose and nothing happened, except it felt very sore, as did my throat. The soreness persisted over Christmas and I had to use my handkerchief a lot. My grandson remarked on the scabs around my mouth and nostrils." The gas from the throwaway lighter seems to have somehow got inside her nose and throat and ignited. What would have happened if she had not closed her nose and mouth? Would the burning gas have gone out anyway? Or could it have been the beginning of Spontaneous Combustion?

We have seen a case in which a teenager burst into flame just after she had stopped dancing. Jenny Randles suggests that this might be due to the fact that some human beings can build up a far higher charge of static electricity than others. Jacqueline Priestman of Stockport, Cheshire, was an example. She was always receiving electric shocks when she touched metal. Electrical devices in her house were always blowing their fuses or burning out – two dozen vacuum cleaners among them. A researcher from Oxford, Dr Michael Shallis, had been studying people who had far more static electricity in their body than most and connected Mrs Priestman up to his instruments. They told him that she had over ten times the normal level of static electricity in her body and that she was blowing fuses by discharging a kind of small lightning bolt. A change of diet – to large quantities of green vegetables – had the effect of curing her. Which leads to the speculation – could an excessive diet of alcohol allow the body to build up large quantities of static electricity, until it somehow started an internal fire?

Undoubtedly, it *is* possible for human beings to "overheat." Jenny Randles cites the case of a little boy, aged four, called Tong Tangjiang, of the Hunan province in China, who often became so hot that he set his clothes on fire. Even when naked, he was able to burn a couch and a mattress. His doctor concluded that the child built up enormous levels of electricity in his body and that this was somehow connected with his age. But he was able to assure the child's parents that the phenomenon would probably pass away – problems of this sort seldom last for very long. The interesting question is what exactly was there in Tong's normal growing process that caused him to generate such heat? Was he simply passing through a process that happens to all growing children – but which, in his case, had got out of hand?

In a nineteenth-century bestseller called *The Night Side of Nature* (1849), Mrs Catherine Crowe describes the case of Angelique Cottin, a 14-year-old French girl, who was weaving silk at an oak frame in January 1846, when the frame began to plunge about. All the other girls retreated to the far side of the room and then returned one by one. The frame remained still until Angelique returned and then began to jerk violently again. Her family assumed it to be a devil and tried to have her exorcised but the priest was inclined to believe it to be a physical phenomenon. He was probably right.

The disturbances became less violent if she was standing on a carpet or waxed cloth. Moreover, her "field of force" did not affect metal. But "organic" objects – even a heavy stone trough – would rear like a frightened horse if her apron touched them. When she was tired, the effects diminished. The disturbances went on from mid-January until April and then gradually died away.

Mrs Crowe mentioned several other cases and added, "Many somnambulistic persons are capable of giving an electric shock; I've met with one person, not somnambulistic, who informs me that he has frequently been able to do it by an effort of will." She goes on to describe the case of Mlle Emmeric, sister of a professor at Strasbourg, who became "electrified" as the result of a bad shock and which also made her become a sleepwalker. Her body "became so surcharged with electricity that it was necessary for her relief to discharge it; and she sometimes imparted a complete battery of shocks to her brother and her physician and whoever was near."

Researcher Max Toth gave a lecture in 1972 in which he listed many cases of "human electric batteries." "The first recorded case dates back to 1879. A 19-year-old girl [Caroline Clare] living in Ontario, Canada, after recovering from an unknown illness symptomized by convulsions, not only discharged electricity but also appeared to have electromagnetic properties. Any metal objects which she picked up would adhere to her open hand and would have to be forcibly pried away from her by another individual.

"Nine years later, in Maryland, a 16-year-old boy with similar electromagnetic properties came to the attention of scientists at the Maryland College of Pharmacy, because of his ability to suspend iron and steel rods, half an inch in diameter and twelve inches in length, from his fingertips. The boy could also lift a beaker of water filled with iron filings merely by pressing three fingers against the side of the container. An audible clicking would occur when he pulled one of his fingers away.

"Perhaps the most impressive of these cases was that of a 14-year-old girl in Missouri [Jennie Morgan of Sedalia] who, in 1895, suddenly seemed to turn into an electric dynamo. When reaching for metal objects, such as a pump handle, her fingertips gave off sparks of such high voltage that she actually experienced pain. So strong was the electricity coursing through her body that a doctor who attempted to examine her was actually knocked on to his back where he remained unconscious for several seconds. To the young lady's relief, her 'shocking' ability eventually began to diminish and had vanished completely by the time she was 20.

"In all of the above mentioned cases, the strange electrical phenomenon was at its height in the early part of the day, diminishing in power as the day waned. It was also, in all of the cases, entirely uncontrollable and involuntary."

Another Missouri teenager, Frank McKinistry, developed an electrical charge during the night and lost it slowly as the day wore on. Perhaps the most interesting thing about his case is that when highly charged *his feet stuck to the ground*, so that walking became immensely difficult.

In the book *Fire From Heaven* (1976), Michael Harrison writes of the research of an American doctor, Mayne R. Coe Jr, who was interested in the subject of telekinesis – mind over matter. Coe was able to move aluminum strips pivoted on the points of needles by moving his hand over them – this was obviously due to some natural physical magnetism. He began various yoga exercises in an attempt to develop his bioelectricity. Sitting in an easy chair one day, he felt a powerful current passing downwards from his head throughout his body – he thought it was high voltage but low amperage. He suspended a cardboard box from the ceiling on a length of string and found that he could cause it to move from a distance – when the room was dry – of as much as eight feet. He then charged his body with 35,000 volts direct current (using an electric current), and found that he could move the box in exactly the same way. This seemed to prove that he was, in fact, generating a high voltage current with his mental exercises. He also went up in an aeroplane to an altitude of 21,000 feet (where the air was extremely dry), and produced electric sparks after he had charged his body up to 35,000 volts. Coe theorized that this could explain the phenomenon of levitation – when the yogi's body floats off the ground – with the positively-charged human body repelling the negatively-charged earth.

According to Dr Coe, each human muscle cell is a battery and a cubic inch could develop 400,000 volts. (The inventor Nicola Tesla used to demonstrate that the human body can take immense electrical charges – enough to light up neon tubes – provided the amperage is kept very low; one of his favorite tricks was to stand in a darkened room holding a neon tube, which would light up the whole room.)

While this is of no help in explaining Spontaneous Combustion – the whole point of Tesla's experiments was that he did *not* burst into flame – we should note that it is high amperage that can cause "burn-ups." If two 12-volt car batteries are connected by a thin wire, the wire will melt. Even thick wire becomes hot, and this could begin to explain why the surroundings of victims of Spontaneous Combustion are undamaged – they are non-conductors.

Coe was interested in electric eels and, by dissecting them, he noticed that half the eel's body consists of three sets of electricity-generating organs, similar in design to the cells of a storage battery. These are modifications of the lateral muscles, but are larger than normal muscle cells and contain more saline solution. It is these electrical cells that enable the eel to give up to 500,000 shocks over a period of 20 minutes – a five-minute rest is enough to restore it to being able to shock again. It is interesting to note that the eel does not actually have to be in contact with the person it is shocking – it can also shock over short distances.

Dr Coe went on to suggest that perhaps we are all similar to electric eels and that each muscle cell is a battery consisting of potassium chloride and sodium chloride in a saline solution, with poles of protein as acid or base. According to this theory, one cubic inch of such "cell batteries" could generate 400,000 volts. Provided that the amperage – whose heating effect is destructive on human tissues – can be kept harmlessly low, the body (according to Dr Coe) may take charges of up to a million votes – enough energy to light many electric lamps.

But the case of Frank McKinistry reminds us that the answer may be something more than simple electricity. McKinistry's feet stuck to the earth in the early part of the day, before he became tired. This is baffling. It would be easy to believe that his feet stuck to metal girders early in the day, but why to the earth? Ordinary soil is not attracted by a magnet and – unless damp – is a poor conductor of electricity. In *Fire From Heaven*, Michael Harrison suggests that the answer could lie in some energy produced by *the earth itself*.

On April 7, 1938, a ship called the *SS Ulrich* was about 50 miles off Land's End in Cornwall and a man called John Greeley was at the helm. It was a calm, bright day, but suddenly the ship began to lurch. The second mate, a man named Phillips, realized that the wheel must be spinning and rushed up to the wheelhouse. There he found John Greeley – or rather what was left of him – lying on the floor "a human cinder." Yet the varnished wood and the wheel were not even scorched and neither was the floor on which Greeley was lying. Doctors would later suggest that Greeley had been struck by a lightning bolt – until the other members of the crew pointed out that there had not been a cloud in the sky.

On the same day, a man called George Turner was driving a lorry near Chester in Cheshire, when it went out of control and rolled into the ditch. When police arrived at the scene of the accident they found that

George Turner, like John Greeley, was "burnt to a cinder" although nothing in the cab of the lorry had been damaged. Even a grease stain on the passenger side of the seat had not ignited.

A third man also went up in flames that same afternoon. His name was Wilhem ten Bruik, an 18-year-old Dutchman who was driving his car near Nijmegen in Holland. Like the other two, he was the victim of sudden Spontaneous Combustion.

Michael Harrison looked carefully at a map showing the south of England and Holland and noticed something of great significance – the three deaths had occurred on the points of an equilateral triangle, whose sides were exactly 340 miles long. On checking the times, Harrison discovered that they all died at virtually the same moment.

Common sense suggests that there *must* be some connection between the three deaths. But what was it? Harrison noted the odd, but otherwise meaningless, fact that the place where all three died began with a U – John Greeley on the *SS Ulrich*, George Turner at a place called Upton-by-Chester and Wilhem ten Bruik at Ubbergen, Holland.

But is it conceivable that the earth itself discharged energy in a triangular pattern? In the book *Ablaze!*, Larry Arnold goes further and suggests that the answer may lie in the lines of force that run across the landscape, which an Englishman called Alfred Watkins referred to as "leys." According to Watkins, the English landscape was criss-crossed by long, straight routes that ran for dozens – sometimes hundreds – of miles across the country. He thought they were probably some kind of trade route, but it seems strange that their makers should take the trouble to keep them so straight when it would have been much easier to allow them to meander around hills instead of going over them.

It was in the 1960s that a student of ley-lines, called John Michell, suggested that these are actually lines of magnetic force and that they often run between sacred places – for example, circles of standing stones, megaliths, ancient barrows, and churches (which are very often built on pagan sites as if the earth itself was somehow regarded as "sacred").

Larry Arnold devotes some of the book to accounts of strange fires and lights on the earth's surface, particularly those associated with earthquakes – for example, in the great earthquake of November 2, 1931, at Kamakura, Japan, hundreds of witnesses observed "rays of bluish searchlights pointing upward from below the horizon." After the earthquake of 1872 at Cerro Gardo, California, witnesses saw sheets of flames, like vast torches, on the sides of the Inyo Mountains.

On the evening of February 6, 1955, a tremendous fire began to blaze on the south ridge of the Santa Catalina Mountains near Tucson, Arizona, with flames that were thought to be 30 or 50 feet high. What was so puzzling was that the residents of Tucson knew that there were no forests up there to create such a blaze. One reporter commented, "There wasn't enough tinder up there to keep a fire going for an hour." But the blaze burned out 1,000 square yards and the earth was scorched two or three inches below the surface at some points. "It looked like someone blasted the area with a giant blow-torch." This, suggests Arnold, is some form of "telluric electricity," in other words, some force from the earth.

Alfred Watkins noted how often places called Brent (which is Old English for the word "burnt") were situated along ley-lines. The Cambridge don, Tom Lethbridge, suggested that megaliths – standing stones – have been pushed into the earth to mark these high-energy points. Moreover, the stones are often used for healing which seems to suggest that they can actually conduct some force from the earth. They might be compared to needles stuck in acupuncture points on the earth's surface. Arnold went on to suggest that ley-lines may be what he called "fire-leynes" – punning on the American expression "fire-lane," a path cut through woodland or countryside which fire engines can use in the event of a blaze.

Arnold took a large map of the British Isles, noted dozens of points where cases of Spontaneous Combustion had occurred and then realized how many of them fell on straight lines joining several such spots. He noted no less than ten cases of Spontaneous Combustion and mysterious fires breaking out along one 400-mile leyne on the east coast of England.

Arnold also discovered that no less than four of these "fire-leynes" ran through the city of Hull. When he was giving a lecture in England, a woman from Hull told him that when she was a child, her mother insisted that the front and the back doors to their ground-floor hallway – which ran the length of the house – should remain open on two days of the year or their house would catch fire.

While Larry Arnold was in England, he investigated

several of the "fire-leynes" which he had traced on his map and studied mysterious fires that had broken out on them. He even discovered one that no one had ever heard of. When he called on John J. Shenton, the Fire Brigade Commander of Lincolnshire, Shenton at first dismissed the whole idea of Spontaneous Human Combustion. Then, as Arnold showed him photographs of well-known cases, Shenton suddenly became thoughtful. He recollected an incident that had happened in the fall of 1972, in a small village called Kirkly-on-Bain. A 79-year-old man, regarded as an eccentric hermit, lived in a hut full of old newspapers and other substances that were highly combustible (like old rags and old clothes), with oiled paper over the windows instead of glass. When the old man had not been seen for two days, constables went to check. All that remained of the hermit were his feet and the upper torso, including the head. The rest had been burnt to ash. There was a heavy layer of greasy soot around the upper walls of the hut but no smell of burnt flesh. The fire officer was baffled by the fact that the bones had also been reduced to ash – which, as we have seen, takes an enormously high temperature. Yet all the newspapers and old rags remained completely untouched. Shenton conceded, as he thought about the case again, that the idea of Spontaneous Human Combustion began to make sense.

However, the earth-force theory also runs into certain problems. John Greeley was incinerated when he was at sea and both George Turner and Wilhem ten Bruik were inside vehicles with rubber tyres. If the "telluric force" is some form of magnetism, then rubber certainly ought to act as an insulator. And what about victims of SHC who live in second-floor flats or even higher? Presumably, the building ought to insulate them from the earth-force. But Arnold has another theory which is equally fascinating. He thinks that some cases of Spontaneous Human Combustion might be connected with UFOs – or flying saucers.

On December 11, 1979, Melvin and Naomi Anderson thought they saw a UFO outside their trailer in Bodfish, California. Two days later, they woke up lying paralysed on the floor and were unable to move. They remained there for another day before neighbors discovered them and took them to hospital. As they lay paralysed, Melvin Anderson had complained to his wife of "burning up inside" but they were both burned on the outside as well. Naomi had severe burns on her left thigh and hip. Melvin was in a worse condition, with a one-and-a-half inch burn on the top of his head and other burns across his back and on his heels. He, like Naomi, had a burn on his left hip and in his case, it went down to the bone.

Doctors could not identify the cause of the burns and investigation of their trailer offered no clues. As the couple recovered, however, their memory of the UFO began to return and they thought they had been taken aboard. That, unfortunately, is the end of the story as reported in local newspapers.

The possibility of UFO abduction has been the subject of many books since 1982, when *Missing Time* by Budd Hopkins described a number of cases in which people gradually remembered being abducted and taken on board alien spacecraft. In fact, the first well-known case had taken place as far back as September 1961, when a couple named Betty and Barney Hill were returning from a holiday in Canada. They stopped their car as a strange-lighted object flew overhead. They arrived home two hours later than they should have done and, under hypnotic regression, recalled being taken on board by "aliens" and subjected to medical examination. Reports of such cases have become increasingly common and today there are hundreds – perhaps thousands – of cases of people who believe that they have, at some time, been abducted and then had their memory erased by the kidnappers.

On December 29, 1980, Betty Cash was driving near Huffman in Texas, with two friends called Vickie and Colby Landrum. At about 9.00 p.m. they saw a great diamond-shaped object at the height of the trees hovering in front of them. It was bright and making a great deal of noise. Flames were shooting from it – so much so that the car became insufferably hot. They thought that they saw Chinook helicopters escorting the object. The car's engine failed and Betty Cash got out. When the object had vanished, their car wouldn't start again – although the handle was so hot that she had to use a cloth to open the door. Later, Betty began suffering severe pains in her head and neck and her eyes swelled. She was apparently suffering from radiation sickness, lost a great deal of her hair and finally developed breast cancer that led to a mastectomy. The other two in the car also suffered hair loss and swelling in the eyes and face.

It has been suggested that the UFO in this case was some secret of the American military and that it behaved like a nuclear reactor. But there have been many other cases in which witnesses have suffered burns or radiation sickness from UFOs. On December 4, 1988, a police officer named A.P. Jones was suddenly blinded by a white light as he drove near Philadelphia. Squinting through the windshield, he saw a giant circular UFO "like a frisbee," about 75 feet in diameter, hovering in the air. He said that the air seemed to be charged with electricity. After ten minutes, during which the UFO rocked back and forth, it suddenly sped away to the east. When he reported it back at headquarters, another policeman said that he had also seen the UFO.

During the next 24 hours, Jones began to suffer from radiation sickness and burns – areas of his skin that had been exposed to the light began to look as if badly sunburned and he suffered from nausea and swollen eyes. It took two weeks for the effects to wear off.

Arnold is not suggesting, of course, that UFOs are responsible for cases of Spontaneous Combustion – merely that there seems to be an interesting possible link and that if we understood UFOs better, we might also discover the key to Spontaneous Combustion.

He cites the case of Marrianne Leith of Hyde Park, New York, who in April 1993 wrote to describe a series of strange encounters in her life – traumatic sightings of UFOs, electrical surges through her entire body, spontaneous scars over half her body, an ability to "make electricity go whacky as I go near it." She added, "I get burns all over my body. What's wrong?" Was this, Arnold wants to know, the same kind of problem that manifests itself in Spontaneous Human Combustion?

In March 1978, a young British service engineer driving home at night, encountered what he called "a glowing mass of energy." He thought that it resembled some kind of human figure. It drifted across the road in front of him and began discharging "energy beams" into his car. His overloaded radio receiver exploded, his watch stopped and would never work again on his body and his fingers showed the "sunburn" effect of radiation. Jenny Randles and Peter Hough investigated this case and were convinced that he was telling the truth. Two years later, the young man died after contracting multiple cancers. Again, as in the case of Betty Cash, it seems highly probable that this was a result of the strange encounter. It also seems clear that the energy had some effect on his body, since the watch would not work whenever he wore it – although it worked perfectly when someone else put it on.

Jenny Randles also tells of a case involving a man at Halewood on Merseyside, England, who was returning from night duty in a car plant in December 1979, when a white "balloon-like" mass floated towards him along a deserted path and drifted close by. The hair on his neck began to tingle and when he arrived home, his wife noted that his hair was literally standing on end and that there were goose-pimples all over his arms. Jenny Randles mentions that the charge remained in his body for 48 hours before it gradually leaked away and he returned to normal.

She mentions another case that occurred in Nelson, Lancashire, at 3.10 a.m. on March 9, 1977, when two night-shift workers were returning to a factory. They saw a kind of mass of swirling light emerge from a cloud above Pendle Hill and the engine and the lights of their vehicle immediately failed. Again, their hair stood up on end. When the strange light moved away, the car engine and the lights began to work. The radiation made their eyes water and also gave them a severe headache.

An engineering student from Hampshire told Jenny Randles of a strange experience he had in June 1935. He was working on a farm at Osmaston, Derbyshire with two friends and at about 11.00 p.m. they were walking towards the road to catch a late bus. There was a crunching sound behind them, as if someone was approaching, and then an invisible field of energy literally passed right through them. He said that they felt a kind of "clamminess" and that their hair stood on end. For a moment, their muscles became so paralysed that they could not walk.

This same engineer told Jenny Randles that three years later, in August 1938, he was cycling up the slope of Glen Almond near Dunblane, in Scotland. Suddenly, he became aware of a dark swirling cloud like a tornado and felt an oppressive sensation. Within moments, this "whirlwind" was surrounding the man on his bicycle and a high-pitched noise filled his ears. A moment later it had passed on. Some people might be tempted to look for supernatural explanations but the student seemed to be convinced that he was simply dealing with some strange force field of an electrical nature. The conclusion drawn by Jenny Randles is that nature is full of peculiar electrical forces which we do not even begin to understand.

But are we correct in trying to explain – or at least

understand – Spontaneous Combustion in terms of forces *outside* us? Might it not be more sensible to begin the search by looking inside? When human beings can turn into magnets or "electric eels," it is obvious that we possess some peculiar powers which we do not even begin to suspect.

In the 1840s, a German chemist called Baron Karl von Reichenbach became interested in people who seemed to have the power to see colors around the ends of magnets. All of them saw a brilliant reddish glow from the south pole and a bluish glow from the north. A girl called Miss Novotny suffered from what was then called "neurasthenia" – or over-sensitive nerves – so that she could not bear any kind of strong light; even a candle was too much for her. But when Reichenbach uncovered the ends of a horseshoe magnet in the dark, she immediately saw colors glowing around its poles. Even when she was sitting with her back to him, she could tell when he had uncovered the magnet. Moreover, when he brought the magnet close to her skin, her flesh stuck to it as if it were made of metal. He tried other "sensitives" with magnetized crystals. The "sensitives" saw the same glow around them in the dark. When he tried unmagnetized crystals, these also worked. When he drew a huge crystal down the patient's arm, she felt a pleasant sensation like a cool breeze. Drawn the other way, it produced a not entirely pleasant warmth. He tried it on a scientific colleague and even the colleague agreed that he felt the same thing.

Obviously, the force in crystals could not be ordinary magnetism. So Reichenbach called it "the odic force."

He became convinced that he had discovered some force that was connected with life – his "sensitives" could see "the odic force" in human beings when they were in a dark room, streaming from the ends of their fingers. (Other people call this the "aura.")

Reichenbach published his researches in a book called *Researches in Magnetism* (1848), and it was hailed as an important contribution to science. But after a while, his fellow scientists began to attack it as total nonsense and before long, they were dismissing him as a crank. (In fact, he was a distinguished chemist and the discoverer of creosote.)

Around the turn of the twentieth century, a London doctor called Walter J. Kilner, who worked at St Thomas's Hospital in London, pursued his own investigations into "the odic force." If it really existed – and was not simply some kind of a delusion induced in Reichenbach's patients by suggestion – then it ought to be possible to see it. Kilner tried placing his patients against black backgrounds and then looking at them through various dyes sealed between two glass plates. He declared that, under these conditions, it was quite easy to see that the human body is surrounded by a kind of envelope of energy that seems to have three distinct layers. The innermost layer he thought was made up of some kind of fine matter, while the other two layers – which extend to well over a foot from the human body – seem to be made of energy. By waving magnets near them and watching the way they change, he was convinced that the human aura *is*, as Reichenbach thought, sensitive to magnetism. Kilner devised a pair of goggles through which, he claimed,

A fireball (possibly ball lightning) seen during a storm in Salagnac, France, in September 1845

any person could quite easily see the human aura. Now virtually all civilizations in the world have claimed that the human body is surrounded by a kind of subtle energy. Many saints have been seen, by their followers, to be surrounded by a halo – sometimes a rainbow-colored "glory."

Like Reichenbach, Kilner was regarded as a crank by his colleagues and few people took him seriously at the time of his death in 1920. But in 1939, Professor Semyon Kirlian was visiting a hospital in Krasnodar in the Soviet Union, and stopped to watch a patient receiving treatment from a new high-frequency generator. As glass electrodes were brought close to the patient's skin, there was a tiny flash not unlike the flash in a neon tube when you turn on the light. In a neon tube, the flash comes from the presence of a gas which is charged by the electric spark. What, wondered Kirlian, was being "charged" by the high-frequency electrode? The obvious way to find out was to try to photograph it. So Kirlian and his wife, Valentina, set up two metal plates to act as electrodes and placed a photographic film on one of them. Then he put his hand between the plates and turned on the current. The result was painful – if the plates had been closer together, a high voltage electric spark would have leapt between them – but when the photograph was developed it showed Kirlian's hands surrounded by a strange glowing corona. When a leaf was photographed between the plates, it showed hundreds of dots of energy and small flares of energy exploding around its edges. When the stem of a newly-cut flower was used, the photograph showed sparks flowing from the stem like a little shower. Strangest of all, when a torn leaf was placed in the machine, the photograph seemed to show the pieces that had been torn away. A dead leaf showed no sparks or flares.

When these results finally leaked through to Europe, about 40 years later, they caused widespread excitement and, for a time, Kirlian photography was studied and written about by many scientists. Then, as usual, the skeptics began to dismiss the whole thing as a purely electrical phenomenon and after the 1970s, Kirlian photography was virtually forgotten.

In 1939, the same year that Semyon Kirlian stumbled upon his discovery, an eminent Freudian psychologist, Wilhelm Reich, startled and enraged his colleagues by announcing that he had discovered a new form of energy unknown to physics – the vital energy which regulates the health of living creatures. He called it "orgone energy."

Reich had always been particularly fascinated by Freud because of his sexual theory. Reich felt that the energy that human beings experience in the sexual orgasm is a pure form of the life force – sheer vital energy – and he believed that most of our illnesses are due to the blockage of these sexual energies, which should flow through the body in the same way that blood flows through our veins. He came to the conclusion that living matter is made up of what he called "bions," tiny cells pulsating with "orgone energy." He claimed that if living matter is made to swell up by being soaked in potassium hydroxide, these bions become quite clearly visible under a microscope. If particles of carbon are dropped into a filtered solution of beef broth and potassium cyanide, the blue "bions" soon begin to appear (according to Reich), and the heavy carbon particles change their nature and become living matter. When "bions" degenerate, said Reich, the result is what he calls T-bacilli, which cause cancer.

On a holiday in Maine in 1940, Reich observed that the stars on the eastern horizon seemed to twinkle more than those in the west, and reasoned that if twinkling is due to the diffusion of light in the atmosphere it should be the same everywhere. Then he observed that there seemed to be blue patches between the stars that flickered and gave off flashes of light. He concluded that "orgone energy" permeates everything, not merely living organisms, and that it causes the flickering of the stars. He even invented a kind of box, made of layers of wood and metal, which he claimed would trap the "orgone energy" like a greenhouse and improve health.

It was this "orgone box" that led to Reich's downfall. He sold the box to anyone who wanted it – which involved shipping it across state lines. Since the box had been denounced by the medical profession as a kind of confidence trick, Reich was finally arrested, thrown in prison for two years and fined $10,000. He died in prison.

We may feel that all these scientists, from Reichenbach to Reich, were simply deluding themselves. On the other hand, their discoveries all sound so similar that there seems a strong possibility that they were all observing the same thing – that human beings are suffused by some kind of unknown energy which is strong when we are healthy and weak when we are unhealthy. The Hindus call this vital energy "Prana" – which means "breath." "Prana" is what makes us alive – it flows through the tissues of our body. If it is blocked or unbalanced, the result is illness and finally death.

The scientific establishment remains doggedly skeptical about the possibility of Spontaneous Human Combustion. In the November 1992 issue of *Nature* (the most influential scientific periodical), science writer Martin Gardner insisted that SHC "is not a burning question. It is not even a question. Not a single textbook on forensic medicine written this century considers the phenomenon a possible cause of death."

Such certainty would seem justified if some scientific body had actually researched SHC, but none have. Simply to say that it looks impossible and therefore *must* be impossible is not scientifically sound. This sort of argument places "debunking" scientists on the same intellectual footing as those "Flat-earthers" who refuse to believe we live on a globe.

The Hindus also state that "Prana" takes the form of an energy called "kundalini," which is not actually a part of our ordinary physical body but of the "astral body" – the part of us which can, under certain circumstances, leave the physical body and look down on it.

The "kundalini serpent," or spirit power, lies coiled at the base of the spine and in conditions of spiritual enlightenment, it can rise upward passing through seven chakras, or energy centers, to the chakra in the crown of the head.

A modern yogi, Gopi Krishna, has described his own experience of the "kundalini serpent" in a remarkable autobiography, *Kundalini, the Evolutionary Energy in Man* (1967). He tells how he first experienced it. "During one such spell of intense concentration I suddenly felt a strange sensation below the base of the spine, at the place touching the seat. The sensation was so extraordinary and so pleasing that my attention was forcibly drawn towards it. The moment my attention was thus unexpectedly withdrawn from the point at which it was focused, the sensation ceased. . . . When completely immersed I again experienced the sensation, but this time, instead of allowing my mind to leave the point where I had fixed it, I maintained a rigidity of attention throughout. The sensation again extended upward, growing in intensity, and I found myself wavering; but with a great effort I kept my attention centered around the lotus. Suddenly, with a roar like that of a waterfall, I felt a stream of liquid light entering my brain through the spinal cord.

"The illumination grew brighter and brighter, the roaring louder, I experienced a rocking sensation, and then I felt myself slipping out of my body, entirely enveloped in a halo of light. . . . I felt the point of consciousness that was myself growing wider, surrounded by waves of light. It grew wider and wider, spreading outward while the body, normally the immediate object of its perception, appeared to have receded into the distance until I became entirely unconscious of it. I was now all consciousness, without any outline, immersed in the sea of light, simultaneously conscious and aware of every point, spread out, as it were, in all directions without any barrier or material obstruction. I was no longer myself, or, to be more accurate, no longer as I knew myself to be, but instead was a vast circle of consciousness in which the body was at a point, bathed in light and in a state of exaltation and happiness impossible to describe."

Gopi Krishna was not entirely happy with the results. He seemed to have released a current over which he had no control and he became exhausted, unable to work, eat or even sit still. Like a high-voltage electric current, Kundalini can apparently be dangerous – it can even bring insanity and death. It took Gopi Krishna no less than 12 years to fully control this energy. He explains that the "Kundalini" energy is basically fiery in nature and says that sometimes he was convulsed with pain, as if red hot needles were piercing his skin, and he became convinced that he was on the point of death.

Dr Lee Sannella, author of *The Kundalini Experience*, tells of a patient who lost awareness while meditating with her hands on the table and who awoke to find burn marks on the table where her hands had been resting. The energy used by "healers" may be of the same nature. One woman who began to practise healing discovered that it caused a warm glow in her fingers. But after she had been resting her fingers on a friend's dress, she discovered she had left scorch marks on it.

So there seems a strong chance that the energy we are speaking about in Spontaneous Combustion may be some unknown energy which human beings are capable of generating.

But it is a case cited by Vincent Gaddis, in his *Mysterious Fires and Lights* (1967), that seems to offer some of the most interesting clues. On September 18, 1952, in Algiers, Louisiana, a lady named Mrs Stalios Cousins observed smoke coming from the apartment above her own and called the fire brigade. The firemen broke in and found the burning body of a man, which they smothered with blankets. Lieutenant Louis Wattigney said, "The man was lying on the floor behind the door, and he was a mass of flames. Not another blessed thing in the room was burning." What puzzled him was that there was no source of fire in the room – no matches, no oil, not even evidence that the man was a smoker. On the other hand, there was a great deal of blood on the kitchen floor.

The burned man was Glen B. Denney, the 46-year-old owner of a foundry at nearby Gretna. Police learned that he had been depressed about personal problems and had been drinking heavily. When seen alive for the last time, he was suffering from the alcoholic "shakes." The coroner's office declared that Denney's death had been due to burns, but that the arteries in both wrists and ankles, had been severed. He had been alive at the time when he was burning because there was a large amount of carbon in his lungs. So it appears that Denney had actually been in the process of killing himself by slashing his arteries when, suddenly, he began to spontaneously combust – at least, the fact that nothing else in the apartment was even scorched sounds typical of Spontaneous Combustion. The final verdict was suicide but the coroner had to admit that he had no idea of what had caused the burning. He thought it might be kerosene, but there was no kerosene in the room.

Gaddis quotes another interestingly similar case which we noted in the last chapter. On the evening of Sunday, December 13, 1959, a man named Billy Peterson, 27-years-old, drove to his house in Pontiac, Michigan, and set about committing suicide by attaching a pipe to the car's exhaust. 40 minutes later, a passing motorist noticed smoke coming out of the parked car (which was in a garage), and called the firemen. Billy Peterson was found dead on the front seat and a patch of upholstery had been ignited by the end of the pipe attached to the exhaust. Peterson's face and arms were badly burned and by the time they got him to hospital, he was dead. Firemen said that the heat in the car had been great enough to melt a plastic statue on the dashboard. Gaddis writes, "It was the condition of Billy's body at the hospital that startled and puzzled the doctors. The victim's back, arms and legs were covered with third degree burns. His left arm was so badly burned that the skin rolled off. His genitals had been charred to a crisp. His nose, mouth and ears were burned. Despite this, the hairs on his body, his eyebrows and the top of his head were all unsinged. Even through burned flesh, hairs protruded unharmed.

"The strange thing was that, although the victim was fully dressed, his clothing – even his underwear – was in no way damaged or scorched. Whatever burned Billy Peterson destroyed his flesh, yet left his hair and his clothing entirely untouched." A Detroit newspaper headlined the case, "Possible Torture Killing."

The police theory was that Peterson might have been

undressed, tortured by fire, then dressed again and put back in the car. But the doctors said that it was impossible that, after receiving such injuries, he could have dressed or been dressed by someone else. Detective Robert Wachal, who first suspected murder, later became convinced that Billy Peterson was a suicide.

So, again, we have an extraordinary case in which a man actually in the process of committing suicide suddenly became a victim of Spontaneous Combustion.

Mary Reeser's relatives stated that she was deeply depressed at the time she died of Spontaneous Combustion in her St Petersburg apartment. She had been trying hard to find herself a flat in her home town but had so far failed. On the day of her death, she had spent the afternoon with relatives but had gone home without telling them that she was going – obviously deeply depressed. Ironically, the telegram that alerted her landlady the next morning was to announce that a flat had now been found for her.

Gaddis comments, "Are we all walking atom bombs, subject to a sudden fiery death caused by conditions that can only be guessed? Does this death spring from man's electrodynamic being – turning inward for self-destruction, while in poltergeist phenomena it is projected outward? Who can estimate, who can know the range and extent of man's subtle, inner abilities in rare and abnormal situations?"

He goes on to cite a book called *The Soul of the Universe* (1948), by Dr Gustaf Stronberg, an astronomer on the staff of the Mount Wilson Observatory of the Carnegie Institute of Washington. It sounds oddly like some of the speculations we have already been considering. Stronberg, according to Gaddis, believed that modern science had failed to offer any comprehensive explanation of man's place in the cosmos. His research project was aided by many major scientists such as Sir Arthur Eddington and even Einstein (who wrote an introduction).

Stronberg begins by pointing out that all matter is composed of atoms which in turn are made of smaller particles. In fact, these particles are (according to quantum physics), basically waves. "Thus they are cores or points of energy concentration rather than independent entities." Stronberg suggested a realm or dimension that exists beyond our senses, and that the world we actually see is merely a kind of reflection of this *reality*. (These views have been echoed by many poets and scientists, from Goethe to David Bohm.) This underlying reality is of a non-physical or quasi-physical nature. "From it emerges fields of force or energy that are the pattern-molds that form all living things – men, animals and vegetation. . . . They are the organizing principles of all life and determine whether a fertilized ovum will produce a human being or a horse or a dog." He believed that the electromagnetic fields in all living things discovered by Dr Harold S. Burr and his associates were part of these energy patterns.

Stronberg wrote, "Our nerve cells seem to be the links which connect our physical brain with the world in which our consciousness is rooted. At death our 'brain field' is not destroyed . . . . it disappears, apparently falling back to the level of its origin." Gaddis comments that since our memories are "engraved" in this force field, he believes that after death we can probably recall them when our minds are no longer blocked by matter.

Gaddis goes on, "Man's electromagnetic being can be considered as a force field intermediary between the physical world and this more refined, subtle world, serving as a pattern and organizing field for the physical body and brain. Through the brain, sensations pass to a directing consciousness and a memory repository in the emergent energy structure beyond. The 'real man' therefore exists beyond our senses; our physical body and brain are our instruments." In other words, what Stronberg is suggesting is a kind of electrical theory of life, which means that our usual notion of physical reality is fundamentally mistaken. Modern physics supports him on this point.

Gaddis's last chapter is entitled, "Suicide – subconscious style." In other words, he considers many cases of Spontaneous Combustion to be cases in which the unconscious mind has somehow directed the electrical energies of the human body into dangerous channels – which the Hindus claim can happen with the "Kundalini" force.

Now, obviously, this fails to explain the strange death of the two Kirby twins in Sowerby Bridge in Yorkshire. Yet what makes that case so bizarre is the fact that two small girls burst into Spontaneous Combustion in different parts of the town at the same moment. Clearly this is not an ordinary case of Spontaneous Combustion. There is something completely incomprehensible involved here, and it seems likely that we shall never be able to understand the nature of Spontaneous Combustion until we recognize that "something incomprehensible" may be involved. Theories that try to reduce it to a purely physical phenomenon – with the body burning like a candle – simply fail to get to grips with the problem.

The present book certainly cannot propose any totally convincing solution to the mystery. But this is largely because we simply lack the kind of knowledge needed to understand it. What are these unknown energies theorized by Reichenbach, Kilner and Reich? They were derided and then forgotten because the science of their time wanted a purely material explanation for the things they observed. They would have replied that a purely material explanation cannot possibly extend to cover all the facts.

In the 1970s, an American professor of aerospace sciences at Princeton University, Dr Robert Jahn, began a series of fascinating experiments with a device called a random event generator. (They are also called random number generators.) By relying on some unpredictable process like radioactive decay, this generator will produce a string of random numbers in binary form – they might read 1,2,1,2,2,1 . . . . and so on. It has been described as a kind of automatic coin flipper. And if a coin is flipped enough times, it will always produce exactly the same number of heads as tails.

Jahn and his associate, Brenda Dunne, asked volunteers to sit in front of their random generator and try to concentrate to make it produce large numbers of either heads or tails. Over hundreds of thousands of trials, they discovered that the volunteers could in fact have a definite – if small – effect on the generator's output. Moreover, the people who were able to produce these effects were not specially trained "psychics," but ordinary people who were simply brought in from the street. What they were proving is that *the mind can actually influence physical reality*.

This is completely contrary to everything that science has believed for the past three centuries, but Jahn has made an important start in placing it all on a scientific basis. He has shown that the mind can actually play a real part in influencing the events around us. And if the mind can exercise this kind of power over a machine, then what are its powers over the body that actually houses it? Every doctor knows that a patient's health is dependent, to some extent, upon his state of mind – that depression can produce bad health and that a sudden burst of optimism can cause a total recovery.

In other words, the answer to the problem of Spontaneous Combustion may lie in the mind itself. When we begin to understand this, then we shall be on the threshold of new discoveries and a new kind of science. And when this new science exists, we may finally have a chance of understanding the nature of Spontaneous Human Combustion.

6

The Mystery of Ball Lightning

On July 5, 1852, a man who lived on the fourth floor in a block of flats in Paris heard a sound like a thunderclap. A large glowing ball, about the size of a human head, emerged from the fireplace, pushing aside the guard that covered it and – according to his own report – darted towards him "like a cat." He quickly moved his feet away as the ball moved to the center of the room. He noticed that it gave off no heat in spite of the bright glow. After that, it rose up off the floor and went back to the fireplace and floated up the chimney. There was a loud explosion from the roof. When this was investigated, it was discovered that the "fireball" had exploded causing a great deal of damage.

In 1890, a great many of these luminous globes were seen in France and reported. The French Academy of Sciences decided to hold a meeting about them, but at the end of the reading of the various reports, a member of the Academy stood up and remarked that all this should be taken with a pinch of salt since the observers must have been suffering from optical illusions. In the heated discussion that followed, everyone agreed that the observations, made by uneducated peasants, were unreliable. At this point, the former Emperor of Brazil (a foreign member of the Academy) stood up and deeply embarrassed everybody by stating that he had himself seen ball lightning.

We have mentioned elsewhere in this book how the great chemist, Lavoisier, went to investigate an account of a meteor which had fallen out of the sky and declared that the witnesses must have been mistaken, because lumps of stone did not fall from the sky. This seems to be typical of the closed minds of scientists. As late as the 1970s, they were still denying the reality of ball lightning. One scientist who worked in the Cavendish Laboratory in Cambridge, who had argued that ball lightning did not and could not exist, was asked what he thought now a globe of lightning had actually been seen to bounce down a corridor in the Cavendish during a storm and exit through a window at the far end. His reply was, "Well, I didn't see it myself."

In the 1970s, one Canadian scientist, Edward Argyll, came up with, what is regarded as, a particularly convincing theory. He pointed out that when lightning strikes the ground, it creates such a bright flash that anyone who sees it will have a persistent afterimage. It is this afterimage, Argyll claimed, that people mistake for ball lightning. In other words, it is an illusion. Argyll pointed out that the various properties attributed to ball lightning would be explained if it was simply an optical illusion – properties like being able to pass through walls or window panes or even metal screens.

Asked what he thought of cases where ball lightning had actually left evidence of its presence – as when it exploded in the Paris chimney – he simply rejected all the evidence declaring, "It would not be unreasonable to categorize these reports as unreliable."

Ball of light less than 8 cm in diameter photographed by Mr M.R. Lyons in early summer 1972 in the Derbyshire hills, England

It would be interesting to know what he thought of the evidence of a Staffordshire housewife, who on August 8, 1975, was in her kitchen during a violent thunderstorm when a flaming sphere of light appeared over her cooker. It came towards her making a strange rattling sound and moved too quickly for her to dodge out of the way. "The ball seemed to hit me below the belt and I automatically brushed it away. Where I touched it there was a redness and swelling on my hand. It seemed as if my gold wedding ring was burning into my finger." The ball exploded with a bang and scorched a small hole in her skirt but otherwise left her undamaged.

Another report of ball lightning described how a two-foot ball dug a trench about 100 yards long and over three feet wide in soft soil near a stream, then literally tore away another 75 feet of the stream bed. This led some scientists to suggest that ball lightning might be an atomic reaction. In an article in *The Unexplained* in 1980, Ronald Hyams concluded, "Ball lightning is as much a puzzle today as it was when it was first reported over 1,000 years ago."

It was also in 1980 that Arthur C. Clarke declared in his television series "Mysterious World," "UFOs may . . . . turn out to be caused by some hitherto unknown phenomenon, perhaps like ball lightning, which is totally unexplained (and even denied by some skeptical scientists)."

In Crystal River, Florida, Mrs Clara Greenlee and her husband saw a reddish-orange ball of lightning shoot through the screen of their concrete patio and roll along the floor – it was about the size of a basketball. Mrs Greenlee, who happened to be holding a flyswatter, batted it and the ball exploded with a sound like a shotgun blast. In fact, this was an extremely dangerous thing to do.

Professor James Tuck, who worked on the atom bomb project in Los Alamos, began to study ball lightning in the laboratory. He had heard that it occurred sometimes in submarines as a result of an incorrect manipulation of the switch that took power from the high-powered battery. Tuck tried to investigate it on board a submarine but his attempts were unsuccessful. Then he discovered that there was a submarine battery at Los Alamos – costing $2,000,000 – that he could use for a time. They managed to produce some extremely powerful discharges from the battery but not ball lightning. Finally, as time ran out and the building that housed the battery was about to be destroyed by bulldozers, they decided on the final experiment – they made a small cellophane box round the switch and blew a little methane gas into it. The result was a sheet of flame and a tremendous roar that practically demolished the building, saving the bulldozers the trouble. Fortunately, it had all been photographed and when the films were examined, they discovered a ball of light about five inches in diameter.

It was when it was finally recognized that ball lightning consists of *ionized* gas that the real advance began. An ion is an atom with some of its outer electrons knocked off by collision with other atoms, so that the gas is electrically charged. The great scientist, Nicola Tesla, observed ball lightning in his large coils when he was using a spherical electrode. He noticed that "fireballs" tended to occur when the oscillations of the coils created opposing magnetic fields.

Will-o'-the-wisp at Issy, June 1871

The traditional name for strange lights that hover in the air over deserted places is "will-o'-the-wisp." Ancient folklore stated that these were the little lanterns that mischievous fairies used to lead travellers into swamps or over cliffs. More recent opinion, however, suggests that these lights are wholly natural and are caused by marshes and graveyards releasing combustible and/or phosphorescent gases into the atmosphere.

In *Mysterious Fires and Lights* (1967), Vincent Gaddis questions this rather plausible explanation. He points out that even when decaying matter releases gases like methane or phosphine, the air will quickly disperse the resultant puff. Even if such a cloud was to spontaneously ignite — for which the marsh gas theorists offer no explanation — it would not "dance about" as "will-o'-the-wisps" have regularly been seen to do. Witnesses have said that "although [will-o'-the-wisps] appear to drift at random, they avoid objects and often slip away from spectators." (This last tendency is possibly the origin of the belief that fairy lights deliberately led travellers astray.)

Gaddis tentatively suggests that "will-o'-the-wisps" are more likely, from their behavior, to be some form of electrical phenomenon like ball lightning. Another possibility is that they are some form of poltergeist manifestation, but that line of thought risks taking us back into the realm of the malicious fairies.

A man called P.A. Silberg wrote an account of some of these accidents in submarines that had produced ball lightning. He noticed that the device called a circuit breaker (consisting of two copper blocks with silver plates on the contact surfaces), each had a piece of metal that curved out of them from the contact surface. It looked as if this metal "trumpet" might be responsible for the ball lightning – when the contact is broken, the first thing that happens is an immense amount of electrical energy continues to leap between the two contact plates as they separate. It seemed possible that this created ionized air, which created a kind of vortex or whirlpool between the two curved pieces of metal.

In 1991, Professor Yoshihiko Ohtsuki of Tokyo's Waseda University, announced that he had succeeded in creating an "electric plasma fireball" in the laboratory. When this "fireball" touched a plate covered with aluminium powder, it created beautiful circles and rings in the powder. Ohtsuki suggested that very large "fireballs" might be responsible for the "crop circles" that had been creating so much controversy since 1980. The theory is certainly plausible – the only objection being that, so far, no one has ever witnessed a "fireball" that was more than about three feet across – they usually vary between the size of a tennis ball and a football – and a "fireball" big enough to create a 60-foot circle in the corn would be seen for miles around – and also heard when it exploded.

When a survey was taken of 4,000 NASA employees, it was discovered that a remarkable number of them had seen ball lightning – so many that it pointed to the inevitable conclusion that it was far more common than anybody had supposed – perhaps just as common as lightning actually striking the earth.

So it looks as if ball lightning is created during thunderstorms when opposing magnetic fields come close together. The result is a kind of soap bubble of ionized air which usually only lasts a second or two – at the most two minutes. But the explosions that have been observed prove that these bubbles contain enormous energy.

We can now begin to see why the suggested explanation of many cases of Spontaneous Combustion is ball lightning. But then, no one has ever seen ball lightning incinerating a human being – although it is reported to have caused some bad burns. On the other hand, there is reason to hope that once we understand exactly how ball lightning is created, we might finally begin to understand the strange mechanism of Spontaneous Combustion.

7

Hellfall – Fire from the Sky

The fall of 1871 was hot and dry across the midwestern United States. From June until October the region had suffered a relentless drought. In the prairies to the south and west – from the booming new city of Chicago to the dense forests of northern Michigan – no rain had fallen and in spite of the Great Lakes, humidity was at an all time low. The desiccated atmosphere tasted dusty and harsh, the plants were parched brown and the ever-present wind (which had caused Chicago to be christened "the windy city") offered no relief. The populace, unprepared for a drought lasting into the winter months, could only pray for relief.

At 9.25 p.m. on the evening of October 8, Fire Marshal Williams and his crew were called to a blaze on DeKoven Street in Chicago's lumber district. Although only one barn (belonging to Patrick O'Leary) was on fire, Williams had good reason to fear the conflagration might spread. Only the previous day, four whole blocks of the city had burned down, the wooden buildings burning like dry tinder. As the firemen fought the O'Leary blaze, they noticed the wind beginning to rise and they worked frantically to bring the flames under control before sparks spread it far and wide.

Williams later reported that when the fire was halted "it would not have gone a foot further; but the next thing I knew they came and told me that St Paul's Church, about two blocks north, was on fire." Once again, Williams doused the blaze before it could spread to neighboring buildings but "the next thing I knew the fire was in Bateham's planing-mill."

This was the pattern from then on – the sparks often leaping whole blocks to settle on some distant building. The firemen were familiar with this process but in this case the "leaps" seemed impossibly long. It was almost, said one, as if the sparks were coming down from the sky rather than from the burning houses.

The increasing gale fanned the fires and spread the sparks. Eventually it was strong enough to break the water from the fire hoses into an ineffectual spray. As the number of fires increased, any hope of control was finally abandoned. The Great Chicago Fire was soon engulfing whole districts. People witnessed six-storey buildings reduced to ashes in less than five minutes. The hair, eyebrows and clothes of fire fighters smouldered in the heat. Temperatures reached high enough to melt stone blocks, while several hundred tons of pig iron piled on the riverbank 200 feet from the flames, fused into a solid mass.

While many people streamed out of the city, others, trapped by walls of flame, were forced to take shelter in the cold waters of Lake Michigan. At the same time, thousands of terrified animals penned in Chicago's huge stockyards, broke free and stampeded through the streets adding to the panic and confusion. Many of the scorched and blinded residents of Chicago were convinced that Judgement Day had arrived.

The unprecedented conditions produced freaks of nature, as when the ongoing wall of fire turned due south and ran half a mile *into* the howling gale. Reporters also noted evidence of the spontaneous combustion of buildings – that is, buildings that seemed to burn from the inside. One newspaperman said it looked "as if a regiment of incendiaries were at work. What latent power enkindled the inside of these advanced [distant] buildings while externally they were untouched?" One witness later said that he believed that there was some unknown "food for fire in the air, something mysterious as yet and unexplainable. Whether it was atmospheric or electric is yet to be determined."

For 27 hours the fire burned unchecked. Over 17,500 of the city's tightly packed wooden buildings were destroyed and 100,000 people were made homeless. The value of the lost property was eventually estimated at $200 million – a near unimaginable figure in nineteenth-century America, when a house could be purchased for $50. Yet, incredibly, only 250 bodies were recovered. Even so, as historian Herbert Asbury later pointed out, this figure did not represent the final death toll: "at least as many more were believed to have been consumed by the fire, which in places reached temperatures as high as 3,000°F (1,650°C)." We have earlier noted that this is the temperature of the furnace in a crematorium.

The "Great Chicago Fire" was the worst city blaze in United States history, but it was not the worst fire disaster. The near total destruction of a major metropolis (started, it was rumored, by Mrs O'Leary's cow kicking over a lamp) has, in the history books, rather eclipsed the firestorm that ravaged eight states, destroyed countless acres of farmland, forest and prairie, and killed nearly 2,000 people. It is doubly strange that historians have neglected this disaster, because it took place on the same night as the Great Chicago Fire, across most of the surrounding states.

In the late evening, a little before O'Leary's barn caught fire, a gale began to blow across the prairie from the southwest. Over the next few hours, this cyclone is believed to have started fires across Illinois, Iowa, Indiana, Wisconsin, Michigan, Minnesota and North and South Dakota. Witnesses spoke of torrents of flame cascading from above and suffocating fogs of thick, black smoke that poured from the howling, crimson sky. The luckiest of these stricken states were the Dakotas, Indiana, Illinois (apart from Chicago) and Iowa. Here no human casualties were reported, but the loss of timberland and crops to flashfire was devastating. Near the town of Yankton in South Dakota, a wall of flame 30 feet tall was seen sweeping before the wind as fast as a "fleet horse could run," devouring everything in its path.

Minnesota was even less fortunate. The counties of Carver, Wright, Meecher and McLeod were inundated with flame and the cities of St Paul and Minneapolis were both under dire threat during the night. A total of 50 people were reported killed by burning or suffocation in this state.

Michigan, with its great forests, was half destroyed by fire. To the east of the state between Saginaw Bay and

144

Lake Huron, an area of some 1,400 square miles was reduced to scorched earth. Blazing forests cut off the towns along the shores of this area and their inhabitants were forced to take to the water to escape. (Rescue boats out of Detroit were still picking up survivors several days later.) 11 townships were partially destroyed and 12 more were completely lost in this area alone. 50 bodies were later dug from the ashes.

To the west, down the shore of Lake Michigan, the towns of Muskegon, Manistee, Glen Haven and Holland were set ablaze. The latter two were all but destroyed and, around Holland, over 200 farmsteads saw their land reduced to a burned waste.

In the center of Michigan, the city of Saginaw suffered $100,000 worth of fire damage and the whole of the Saginaw Valley, south to Flint, was set on fire. Only the combined male populations of Midland, Bay City and Lansing managed to keep the blaze in check. Nonetheless, the counties of Gratiot, Iosco, Alpena and Alcona were devastated.

But it was the state of Wisconsin that was hardest hit. An area of at least 400 square miles – between Brown County in the north and Marinette on Green Bay in the south – was devastated with the loss of nine towns and comprising four whole counties. Although this was less than a quarter of the land damage suffered by Michigan, over 1,500 people lost their lives in this area. About half of these were later found not to have burned to death but to have asphyxiated – outdoors in the middle of a hurricane.

In his *History of the Great Conflagration* (published in 1872), James W. Sheahan described the storm's huge swathes of destruction: "The track of the great Sunday night tornado on the west side [of the stricken area] commenced about six miles north of Oconto, extending 15 miles in width, and running parallel 30 miles northward down the bay. The track on the east side commencing in the town of Humbolt, ranged ten miles in width, sweeping northeast 40 miles to Big Sturgeon Bay. The west side district took in the village of Peshtigo, the Sugar Bush settlements, the village of Menekaune, at the mouth of the Menominee, and the Birch Creek settlement, eight miles beyond in the borders of Michigan. All were swept out of existence."

Of 78 inhabitants of the village of Williamsonville, only four survived that night. At the town of Menekaune, dozens of people who could not reach the relative safety of the bay, died amid the blazing houses. At Williamson's Mills almost every member of 14 families perished, 32 people desperately threw themselves down the settlement's well but were all found dead. In the Sugar Bush settlements over 260 people were killed – many were found suffocated, but otherwise unmarked, in areas some distance from the flames.

It was, however, in the town of Peshtigo that the most terrible losses of the night were incurred. In 1871, Peshtigo was a growing metropolis of over 2,000 people. It maintained 15 hotels and shops, several factories and 350 homes. By the morning of October 9, not a building remained.

Survivors later told of a cloudless evening with a wind strong enough to shake the wooden houses. Around 9.30 p.m. a red glare was seen to the southwest, expanding to fill the sky as it approached with the storm. A swelling rumble that soon reached the pitch of continuous thunder accompanied the crimson light. In the last moments before the catastrophe, sharp reports (like distant cannon shots) were heard – these were later identified as explosions of methane as the firestorm passed over neighboring marshes. In the last seconds, the whoosh and crash of igniting and falling trees filled the air, then the storm engulfed Peshtigo.

One survivor gave this description of the first few moments of the destruction: "In one awful instant a great flame shot up in the western heavens, and in countless fiery tongues struck downward into the village, piercing every object that stood in the town like a red-hot bolt. A deafening roar, mingled with blasts of electric flame, filled the air and paralysed every soul in the place. There was no beginning to the work of ruin; the flaming whirlwind swirled in an instant through the town. All heard the first inexplicable roar, some aver that the earth shook, while a few avow that the heavens opened and the fire rained down from above. The tornado was but momentary, but was succeeded by maelstroms of fire, smoke, cinders and red-hot sand that blistered the flesh."

The superheated blast ripped the roofs from the houses, setting them ablaze before they could hit the ground. Unshielded buildings, animals and people exploded into flame where they stood. Even the citizens who were covered from the direct blast of the storm were choked by the black whirlwinds of smoke or suffocated as the burning air seared their lungs. One house on the edge of town was whipped straight up into the air like Dorothy's farmstead in *The Wizard of*

Oz, but this building was not destined to fly over the rainbow. Witnesses said that the walls of flame around the town met to form a dome of fire and that, at about 100 feet above the ground, the flying house burst into flames and was torn to pieces.

After the first onslaught, Peshtigo's firestorm slackened a little. Several firemen even tried to deploy a fire hose but it burst into flames and was reduced to melted rubber before they could start pumping the water. For those who were not already dead or incapacitated, the only hope of survival lay in the Peshtigo River, which ran through the center of the town, but getting there was the problem – landmarks were ablaze and the smoke hung in the air like a blanket. Nowhere in the open was safe as the wild gusts of wind could hurl tongues of fire like a flame-thrower. Finally, those who did not cover their mouths or who took a direct gasp of the superheated air, risked scorching their lungs too badly to take another breath.

Two mobs of terrified people met in the middle of the wooden bridge that spanned the river. In the grim confusion, the groups fought to pass one another, both being convinced that the far side must be safer than the inferno they were trying to escape. As they strove against each other the bridge, which was itself in flames, buckled and collapsed.

One man managed to keep his head in the surrounding panic. Seeing that his sick wife could never make it to the river on foot, he and their five children pushed her, bed and all, out of the house and into the rushing water. They had trouble keeping her head above the surface but the whole family survived.

Those who made it to the river were not out of danger. In those days, when bathing in public was still considered indecent, few men and virtually no women knew how to swim. The flaming, smoke-laden air above the water was difficult to breathe and burning debris was being swept down the current towards the bobbing heads. Since this was a rural community, there were also terrified horses and cows running loose – many people died of a combination of burning, trampling and drowning.

Outside the town, an impenetrable wall of burning woodland blocked the way. Many people sought refuge in the few brick buildings, but these turned into ovens and their calcined bones were later found amid the heat shattered rubble. Only one group, who staggered into the swampy ground to the east, managed to escape by lying flat in the hot, brackish water.

One farmer on the edge of town shot his family and himself before the surrounding flames could close in. In another area, a desperate mother dug a hole in the earth with her bare hands, placed her baby in it, then shielded the child with her own body. She was burned to death – the baby was found unmarked but had suffocated.

In the early morning hours, the firestorm abated. By dawn most of the fires were dying but only because almost everything in the area had burned to ash. Survivors suffering from burns, lacerations and exposure staggered up the riverbank to look across a blackened landscape stretching as far as the eye could see. The final death count in Peshtigo was 1,152.

Because the "Great Chicago Fire" commanded all national attention, it was several weeks before anything other than local help was offered to survivors in the rural areas. The governors of Michigan and Wisconsin were both forced to issue special proclamations begging for assistance. It was months before the terrible damage could be fully assessed – indeed, in some areas, fires continued to burn for over three weeks. Ashes from the conflagration were blown as far eastward as the Azores. The official explanation for the calamity was a windstorm that carried sparks – originally from bush fires in the southern prairies, than from the fires caused by the storm itself.

Yet this theory seemed somehow inadequate. It failed to explain the sheer violence of the firestorm. Over recent centuries, droughts have been recorded world-wide – some going on for decades – but nowhere have high winds and flying sparks created a holocaust like the one that struck the midwest in 1871. Accounts like the one from Peshtigo comment that the very air appeared to be on fire. Witnesses of spontaneously combusting buildings in Chicago could only suggest invisible "incendiaries" or mysterious "food for fire in the air," as a cause. Moreover, the high incidence of death by suffocation, not only outdoors but often far from burning areas, suggested to many that there may have been some deadly quality in the wind itself.

Could there have been any basis for these suspicions? In fact, a number of unexplained heat blasts have been recorded since the Great Midwest Fire. On July 6, 1949, the town of Figueira on the central Portuguese coast was hit by what was described as "an inferno-like blast." It was early morning – the time when most Portuguese housewives were out doing the day's shopping – and few others were about. Suddenly, without warning or obvious cause, the air temperature soared to an unbearable level. A naval officer by the harbor reported a thermometer leaping from 100 to 158°F (38 to 70°C) in only a few seconds.

The firestorm that ravaged the Midwest on October 8–9, 1871, left strange evidence in its wake. Trees were found to have burned down to their deepest roots – a phenomenon unknown to even the most ferocious forest fire. At the same time, people were reduced to heaps of ash in a way similar to the victims of Spontaneous Human Combustion. For example, a heavily built Peshtigo lumberjack was reduced to "a mere streak of ashes, [just enough] to fill a thimble," while three adults, killed on the same spot, left "only enough ashes to fill a two quart measure." Some people, later presumed dead, left "not a trace – [they had] vanished from the Earth," according to Goodspeed's *History of the Great Fires in Chicago and the West* (1871).

Others, escaping the fires, died without a mark upon them or their clothes, apparently by poisoning or suffocation. Yet the coins found in the pockets of some of these unburned victims were discovered to have fused together (temperatures of 1,600 to 2,000°F (871 to 1,093°C) are needed to melt silver and copper – cloth, obviously, burns at a much lower temperature).

The blast was reported to have felt like "tongues of flame." Hundreds of people were knocked senseless, while others prayed in terror or searched fruitlessly for somewhere cooler. Cattle and donkeys panicked and thousands of poultry simply fell dead. The Mondego River, which discharges into the Atlantic at Figueira, steamed and even dried up at several shallow points. The Spanish press reported that in one place "millions of fish died in the mud that was rapidly becoming a sand bed." Then, approximately two minutes after it hit, the heatwave passed like the lifting of a curtain. But the mystery inferno had only moved inland. 30 miles from the coast, the town of Coimbra was roasted a short while later – here the scorching again lasted two minutes before passing, this time for good. No unusual winds, sun-effects or tectonic movements were noted immediately before, during or after the event. It simply came from the clear air over the sea, then vanished.

Some researchers connected the Portuguese heat-blast with somewhat similar events in Spain four years before. The province of Almeria had suffered a plague of bizarre fires beginning on June 16, 1946. Throughout that day, around the town of La Roda, white clothing spread out to dry suddenly burst into flames. This had never been known to happen before nor was any other shade or color of cloth affected.

During the next 20 days, over 300 unexplained fires broke out in the area. Not just laundry but farmhouses, barns, threshing-bins and even the clothes on people's backs burst into flame without visible cause. In almost every case, the object damaged had been white.

A team of government scientists was dispatched to the area, but when they unpacked a box containing their instruments it burst into flame. The rather disgruntled experts eventually reported that the fires might either be the result of "St Elmo's fire" (a harmless and heatless electrical discharge), or underground mineral deposits. The director of Spain's National Geographic Institute connected the two theories when he noted that "the land [around La Roda] is a particularly good conductor of electricity." They could not, however, explain why the area had only recently been plagued by incidents of Spontaneous Combustion if it was naturally prone to them. Obviously, even if they were on the right track, some unknown catalystic force was at work.

The Spanish press reported that on July 5, 1949, a "great column of whirling wind of a luminous brown color struck a small settlement with a violent roar and kindled flames which leapt 30 feet high." This, however, seems to have been the climax of the Spontaneous Combustion plague in Almeria. Several minor fires were reported over the next few days but by July 10 the phenomenon had ceased altogether.

Such stories might remind readers of *Star Wars* orbital lasers and (in the case of the burning wind that struck Peshtigo) the heat blast that devastated Hiroshima after the dropping of the atomic bomb. In fact, at least one ufologist has suggested that the Almeria heat blast might have been due to aliens making yet another unpredictable demonstration of their strange technology. Discounting such unverifiable notions, there is the possibility of freak atmospheric effects – perhaps a very short-lived hole in the ozone layer, which allowed intense solar radiation to reach the planet's surface – or even of another kind of intruder from space. . . .

A few years after the "Great Chicago Fire," Minnesota congressman and author, Ignatius Donnelly, made an interesting observation in his book *Ragnarok*. He noted that Biela's comet, during its close brush with the Earth's gravity field in 1846, had been split into two parts. The shattered comet was due to return in 1866 but, to the astonishment of astronomers, it failed to appear. Then, in November 1872 (just over a year after the Great Midwest Firestorm), it reappeared unexpectedly in a spectacular and meteoric display. All of which might seem irrelevant to the events of 1871, except that the comet was missing its tail during the 1872 visit.

A comet is made up of a "head" of solid ice and a long "tail" of gases, ice particles and space dust resembling the wake of a ship. Donnelly suggested that the 1846 brush with the Earth had detached Biela's tail and that after the split head of the comet had been diverted into a slightly different orbital path, the material of the tail continued orbiting the sun. Donnelly's theory was that, 25 years later, on the night of October 8, 1871, the remains of the tail returned and plunged into the atmosphere over the midwest. The burning, demon wind that ravaged across eight states, he suggested, was a direct result of the atmospheric impact and superheating of a cloud of space debris.

Comets had been feared as harbingers of disaster throughout world history. In recent years, some scientists – such as Fred Hoyle – have suggested the earth may have been seeded with life by cometary impact. Hoyle has raised the question of whether great epidemics like the Black Death might have reached us from outer space. Is it possible that our ancestors also recognized that comets might also bring fire and devastation in their train?

Mystery lights in Texas, September 1986 (copyright James Crocker/Fortean Picture Library)

The mystery sunsets of 1908 bring us to a case in point. The weather during that summer led some religious enthusiasts to predict the end of the world. From early July right into the winter months, the sunrises and sunsets in the northern hemisphere were particularly stunning. These gorgeous Turneresque skies reminded meteorologists of similar atmospheric effects following the tremendous eruption of the Pacific volcano, Krakatoa, in 1883. Yet, no reports of a violent, volcanic upheaval came to the attention of weather stations.

The night skies were also disturbingly bright that summer. In London, it was possible to read a newspaper outdoors at midnight. People took photographs without the aid of flashpower in Stockholm at 1.00 a.m., and in Russia, midnight was as light as an overcast summer's afternoon. Meteorologists recognized the effect as an indication of large amounts of dust that had somehow been released into the upper atmosphere.

Geologists engaged in seismic research offered a clue to the mystery. On June 30, 1908, a tremendous shock was recorded on seismographs worldwide. Yet – unlike earthquakes or volcanic eruptions – there were no preliminary or aftershocks. Nevertheless, the shock wave was intense enough to travel around the planet twice before subsiding. The indicators showed that it had originated somewhere in eastern Russia which further ruled out volcanic activity, since the region is tectonically stable.

No one took much further interest. Even within Russia (then in the throes of social upheaval), few experts showed any inclination to pursue the matter. The detonation had apparently taken place in Siberia, a sparsely populated, forested wilderness – even then used as a dumping-ground for social and political undesirables. It was not until the Great War had been fought and the revolutionaries had overthrown the tsarist regime and executed the royal family, that the new Soviet Academy of Sciences sent somebody to investigate the mysterious detonation.

In 1921, investigator Leonid Kulik came across reports of a major explosion in decade-old Siberian newspapers. Although the accounts were confused and, in places, contradictory, he realized that something incredible had happened in the remote forests on June 30, 1908.

Witnesses quoted in newspapers spoke of a bright white light appearing in the sky just before 7.00 a.m. Over a period of about ten minutes, this lengthened like a comet's tail until a vaporous line seemed to split the sky. Then, when the end of the streak seemed to almost touch the ground, there was a tremendous explosion, which reverberated like artillery fire. About 800 miles from the detonation point, the driver of the Trans-Siberian Express halted his train, convinced that they were derailed. 200 miles away in the village of Nizhne-Karelinsk, heavy clods of turf were shaken from the roofs and some villagers suffered temporary deafness. Men were blown off their horses. Earth tremors were reported from Irkutsk, Tashkent, and even Jena, Germany. Closer to the explosion, witnesses reported painful sunburn on the portions of their bodies facing the explosion, while many houses were knocked flat.

One farmer who was ploughing an open field, even described how his shirt had burst into flame on his back. After the flash and repeated booms of the explosion, a great pillar of black smoke rose high into the sky, fanning out at the top to form a giant, mushroom-shaped cloud.

To Kulik, an expert on meteorites, it seemed clear that the earth had suffered the impact of a large piece of space debris. For the next six years, he studied the event from Moscow – pockets of pro-tsarist "Whites" holding out in Siberia made it dangerous to travel there.

In 1926, a Siberian meteorologist sent Kulik his own calculation of the point where the mystery object exploded – the deeply-forested region called Tunguska. Now Kulik finally persuaded his superiors to allow him to go and investigate. As soon as the Russian winter started to release its grip (early in 1927), Kulik left for Siberia.

The vast Siberian forest is a daunting prospect for even a well-equipped expedition. Frozen solid in winter, during the spring and summer it becomes humid, boggy and infested with mosquitoes. In 1927, the tiny settlements were often hundreds of miles apart and were usually only found on the shores of rivers. Roads and permanent paths were rare to the point of non-existence. There were no maps and, even today, large regions have only ever been surveyed from the air. Kulik penetrated this wilderness on horseback, accompanied by only two local guides from the small town of Vanavara.

Kulik's guides had witnessed the explosion in 1908 and they estimated that the Mekirta River ran somewhere close to the point of the explosion. Rough as it was, this guess was the best they could offer since, in 18 years, no local had risked investigating the area. After a month's hard travel, Kulik's expedition arrived at the banks of the Mekirta in April. And it was at the top of a ridge of hills above the river that Kulik finally found what he had been looking for.

As far as the eye could see, the forest had been totally flattened. The trees behind the ridge had been screened from the blast but, approaching the top, they had been broken-off close to the ground. Beyond the line of hills, the flat boglands had been swept clear of trees as if by a scythe and Kulik noted with awe that every fallen tree lay pointed in the same direction. This, he realized, indicated that the distance from the hills to the horizon – around 12 miles in a direct line – could be, at most, only half of the range of the explosion. No blast of such enormous proportions had been recorded in human history, with the possible exception of the explosion of the volcano of Krakatoa in 1883.

Kulik was inclined to believe that, somewhere out of sight, there must be an enormous crater – perhaps as big as the 600-foot deep meteorite crater of Arizona. He was determined to find it. Unfortunately, the guides had other ideas. The devastation filled them with terror – they thought something supernatural was responsible and were unwilling to provoke it by venturing into its territory. They announced their intention of returning home immediately and all of Kulik's pleas failed to dissuade them. This meant that Kulik had to return to Vanavara with them and see if he could find less nervous guides.

He eventually recruited some fearless Evenki hunters and they left Vanavara on April 30. After days of walking through snow-covered forest, they arrived at the Chambé River (on which the winter ice was just breaking up), and took to rafts which they had constructed on the banks. Surrounded by melting ice floes, they navigated along the flooded river – on one night a raft full of equipment was swept away. Finally, on June 1, Krulik again arrived at the scene of devastation.

At least he had no trouble finding the heart of the explosion – all he had to do was to follow the line of the fallen trees. It took them three days to reach the center, and here Kulik was in for another surprise. Instead of a deep crater, there was merely a natural amphitheater of low hills. All around the "cauldron" (as Kulik christened it), the trees lay pointing away in every direction but in the bowl itself, some trees remained standing – although stripped of bark and badly charred.

Even a cursory investigation revealed that the "cauldron" was not formed by the impact – its hills were rounded by weather. Yet other evidence clearly pointed to an explosion of almost unimaginable size. The expedition had travelled 37 miles from the line of hills above the Mekirta River to the "cauldron." If the blast area was equal on all sides, that meant a devastated area of over 4,300 square miles. Yet here, at the center of this destruction, was a relatively undamaged patch of ground.

The answer to the riddle is rather easier for our post-Hiroshima generation to understand. Anyone who has seen photographs of the ruined, but still erect, buildings that were directly below the detonation of the atom bomb will understand something of the strange effects of an airborne explosion. Kulik, of course, had no such idea but soon realized that the Tunguska object must have exploded before it hit the ground.

Kulik was convinced that the source of the explosion had been a giant meteorite. Such space boulders contain certain characteristic mineral deposits and a large proportion of iron – some identifiable fragments of which should have survived the explosion. Between 1927 and World War II, he returned with four expeditions to search for the meteorite debris that would prove his point. Studying the area around the "cauldron," he noted various deep holes filled with swamp water. These, he believed, were made by chunks of meteoric iron blasting into the ground like bullets.

Kulik's attempts to raise fragments of meteorite from the holes proved exhausting and frustrating. The boggy ground made the draining of the pits virtually impossible and the site's isolation meant that they could transport only the simplest and most portable tools. By the end of the fourth expedition, Kulik had raised nothing more substantial than a tree-stump from any of the "meteor holes." In fact, the pits eventually turned out to be perfectly natural features of the Siberian landscape. During the sub-zero cold of the Russian winter, ice below ground forces its way to the surface in a series of pillars. When the ice melts in spring, water-filled pits remain.

Kulik did, however, record some interesting observations on other effects of the explosion. There was evidence of two waves of destruction that had radiated from the exploding object. The first had been a blast of intense heat, which was followed almost instantly by the concussion blast that scythed down the trees. In 1938, an aerial survey revealed that the devastation was less widespread than Kulik had calculated – only 770 square miles of forest had been destroyed in an oddly irregular blast pattern.

Locals reported that reindeer and wild dogs had suffered skin welts or burns after the explosion – this seemed consistent with the painful "sunburns" suffered by human beings who were less close to its center. The trees that had survived the blast also showed strange side effects. Some had stopped growing altogether, as if held in suspended animation. Others had sprouted up at an accelerated rate.

If Kulik had survived, he would have been deeply interested in the Hiroshima and Nagasaki atom bomb blasts. These explosions (which did not take place on impact, but high above the ground), produced first heat then concussion waves. They also created irregular areas of destruction and soaked everything in gene-deforming gamma radiation. Unfortunately for science, the man who survived the many dangers of the Siberian wilderness was killed in a Nazi prisoner-of-war camp.

Supporting evidence that the Tunguska explosion may have been nuclear comes from post-war research into the area of the blast. One of the central figures in this research has been Professor Alexis Zolotov, who led expeditions in 1959 and 1960. The result of this was a rejection of the two most popular theories – that the Tunguska object was a meteor or a comet. If it was a meteor, why did it explode in the air? (Zolotov estimates about three miles above the ground.) And why is there no sign of its debris?

An exploding comet, on the other hand, would not necessarily leave behind traces, since it is basically a giant snowball and would evaporate. The British scientist, Frank Whipple, and the Russian, I.S. Astapovich, were the first to suggest – in the 1930s – that the Tunguska object might have been a comet, but opponents of the theory soon pointed out that of 120 observatories questioned by the Russians, not one recorded a comet on the trajectory of the Tunguska object in 1908.

Besides, comets travel far slower than meteors and the estimates made by Whipple and Astapovich suggest kinetic energy of ten to the power of 21 ergs per second, the equivalent of about two Hiroshima bombs, while Zolotov worked out that the energy released was about 1,000 times greater. (He estimated the explosion to be about 40 megatons, 2,000 times greater than the Hiroshima bomb.)

Radiation levels taken in the Tunguska area in the 1960s were normal – but that was hardly unexpected after more than half a century. Zolotov concluded, nevertheless, that the Tunguska event was an atomic explosion – not simply because of the abnormal genetic development of some vegetation and of ants and other insects found in the area, but because he found abnormal quantities of radioactive "caesium 137" in the tree rings for 1908. ("Caesium 137" is one of the products of a nuclear reaction.) He also pointed out that atomic explosions have a major effect on the earth's magnetic field and the region around the Tunguska "cauldron" has been described as a "magnetic chaos."

But if it was a nuclear explosion then what caused it? Over 700 eyewitnesses later said that the streak of white vapor that ended with the Tunguska detonation changed course on its way to the ground. Most claimed that it first headed towards Lake Baikal but then turned northward. Charles Berlitz, a well-known student of "anomalies," has suggested that since falling heavenly bodies have never been known to make such a drastic change of course, the Tunguska object may have been an alien spacecraft with a malfunctioning nuclear engine. He goes on to point out that Lake Baikal is one of the largest bodies of fresh water on the planet. Perhaps the aliens had aimed to cool their reactors in the lake, but at the last minute realized that they were not going to make it and directed the craft over uninhabited forest.

A.A. Jackson and M.P. Ryan of the University of Texas have suggested that the Tunguska object might have been a miniature "black hole." These monsters from the space bestiary are formed when the particles within a star collapse under the pressure of their own mass. The result is a gravity whirlpool from which even light cannot escape – hence the term "black hole." Jackson and Ryan's theory suggested that, by some unknown process, a much smaller piece of matter had collapsed to form a pin-size "black hole" (a star-sized "black hole" would have "eaten" our whole solar system), and hit the earth like a high-velocity bullet.

The Russians took this hypothesis seriously enough to investigate the possible consequences of such an encounter. A tiny "black hole" would indeed have created a massive explosion wherever it hit but would have been too small to make an impact crater – just the circumstances found at Tunguska. But then, as Thomas Huxley once noted, a good theory is all too often destroyed by a single cruel fact. In this case, the cruel fact is what police forensics experts call the "exit wound effect." When a projectile strikes a large object it makes a small hole as it enters but, due to inertia, will make a much bigger hole as it exits – taking a lot of material with it. In the case of Jackson and Ryan's "black hole," Iceland and a large section of the north Atlantic would almost certainly have been blasted into the upper atmosphere. Just to be certain, the Soviets checked Icelandic newspapers for June 30, 1908, but not even a small eruption was reported.

Another suggestion put forward by American scientists, as well as by the Russian, Alexander Kazantsev, is that a piece of anti-matter was responsible for the Tunguska explosion. Anti-matter, for all its science fiction connotations, has been proved to exist. Physicists working with giant particle accelerators have managed, through the staging of subatomic particle collisions, to make tiny, short-lived motes of anti-matter. This material has a near instantaneous life span because it is the direct opposite of the "positive" matter of which the universe is made. As soon as matter and anti-matter meet they "cancel each other out," leaving nothing but an explosion of energy and a burst of radiation – again, a situation reminiscent of the Tunguska event. Unfortunately for this hypothesis, there is as yet no evidence that anti-matter can be created outside a particle accelerator. Furthermore, critics of the theory have pointed out that anti-matter would have exploded as soon as it touched the upper atmosphere.

Nevertheless, it is Kulik's meteor theory that continues to be the most popular in scientific circles. It has been suggested that the atmospheric superheating of the outer layers of a large meteor might have reacted with extreme violence with the frozen interior. Whether such a reaction – familiar to anyone who has thoughtlessly poured boiling water into a thick-sided glass – could have been violent enough to flatten 770 square miles of forest is a matter for speculation.

An event on August 10, 1972, adds plausibility to that theory. A fireball "looking like a gigantic welder's torch" tore across the skies of the northern United States and Canada. It took only one-and-a-half minutes to travel from Salt Lake City to Alberta. Its diameter was estimated at only about 13 feet – about a tenth of that of the Tunguska object. But it still had the explosive power of the Hiroshima bomb. Yet instead of ploughing into the earth, its angle of motion meant that it ricocheted off our atmosphere, as a flat stone ricochets off water, and vanished again into space. At a slightly steeper angle, it might have struck Alberta and wiped out its population. The event reminds us that dangerous visitors from space can invade our atmosphere at any moment.

There is one more fact that adds plausibility to Kulik's meteor theory – that every June 30, the earth goes through the Beta-Taurid meteor stream thus producing a meteor shower. Meteor streams are smaller versions of the asteroid belt between Mars and Jupiter. Fortunately, the passing of our planet through a meteor stream generally produces only beautiful firework-like effects.

65 million years ago, a huge meteorite struck the earth in what is now the Gulf of Mexico. A vast cloud of dust and vapor was thrown into the atmosphere, causing a worldwide, climatic change that scientists think brought about the mass extinction of the dinosaurs.

At 11.02 p.m. on November 29, 1996, a three-mile long asteroid passed within 3.3 million miles of the earth travelling at 85,000 miles per hour. This may sound a safe distance, but the fact that the astronomers named the behemoth "Toutatis" (after the Celtic god who threatened to bring the sky crashing down), gives some indication of our close call. If "Toutatis" had been drawn into earth's gravity field, the impact would have made a crater 30 miles across and would have thrown enough dust into the atmosphere to blot out the sun, and would certainly have killed millions of people.

Compared to what might have happened if "Toutatis" had struck us, the Tunguska explosion was almost negligible. Yet, if its trajectory had caused it to arrive a few hours sooner or later, it might have caused one of the greatest disasters in recorded history. On roughly the same latitude as the Tunguska region is Warsaw, Berlin, London, Winnipeg and Vancouver. In fact, along that line of latitude, Siberia was one of the few areas of land where a huge explosion could take place without causing any loss of human life.

The fact that it exploded in the atmosphere was also a striking piece of good fortune for the human race. A meteorite weighing 1,000 tons – which is the size Zolotov estimates – would have thrown enough dust into the atmosphere to adversely affect the weather patterns for the whole planet. Those who enjoyed the glorious sunrises and sunsets of 1908 could scarcely have guessed they had just escaped a mini-ice age.

It is a sobering thought that the giant asteroid, "Toutatis," came within 3.3 million miles of us in 1996 – close enough, some astronomers thought at the time, to pull it on a collision course with the earth.

"Toutatis" is not gone for good, however. Its orbit is due to bring it within only *one million miles* of earth on September 29, 2004. If it is drawn into our gravity-well, we can only hope that it too might spontaneously combust like the mystery object above Tunguska.

Index